D1605777

The future of teacher education

The future of teacher education

Edited by

J. W. Tibble

Emeritus Professor of Education
University of Leicester

Routledge & Kegan Paul
London

First published 1971
by Routledge & Kegan Paul Ltd.
Broadway House, 68–74 Carter Lane,
London EC4V 5EL
Printed in Great Britain by
Unwin Brothers Limited,
Woking and London

ISBN 0 7100 7189 2

Contents

Tables

Abbreviations

A.T.C.D.E.	Association of Teachers in Colleges and Departments of Education
A.T.O.	Area Training Organization
A.U.T.	Association of University Teachers
B.J.E.P.	*British Journal of Educational Psychology*
B.J.E.S.	*British Journal of Educational Studies*
B.P.S.	British Psychological Society
C.N.A.A.	Council for National Academic Awards
E.P.A. (Sch.)	Educational Priority Area (schools)
N.A.S.	National Association of Schoolmasters
N.F.E.R.	National Foundation for Educational Reasearch
N.U.T.	National Union of Teachers
P.G.C.E.	Post-Graduate Certificate in Education
S.S.R.C.	Social Science Research Council
U.D.E.	University Department of Education
U.G.C.	University Grants Committee

This book is intended as a contribution to the current debate about future developments in teacher education. Criticism of teacher education is no new thing, but it has certainly risen to a crescendo in recent years, culminating in demands from various quarters for some kind of national enquiry. As is liable to happen with prayers for rain, the response has been rather more than the askers bargained for: no less than three enquiries have been instituted. First the Select Committee on Education and Science of the last government took teacher education as its next topic and published evidence and interviews with witnesses up to the time of the change of government in June 1970. Then in February 1970, Mr Short, then Secretary of State for Education and Science, invited all Area Training Organizations to undertake surveys of their provision for teacher education and report to him in due course. These surveys are continuing and hope to have some findings ready in time for presentation to the third national review, a Committee of Enquiry instituted by Mrs Thatcher and now meeting under the Chairmanship of Lord James of Rusholme.

As several of the contributors to this book observe, it seems somewhat ironical that this ferment of criticism and enquiry should reach a peak at a time when teacher education flourishes as never before. The Colleges of Education have just completed a remarkable and successful expansion from 27,000 students in 1957 to 116,000 in 1970–1. This has been achieved by the founding of new colleges, the expansion of existing colleges and various expedients in crowding up and double banking. It has been associated with some marked changes in the nature and ethos of the colleges: many single-sex colleges have become mixed, for example; the proportion of students in residence has dropped sharply; the kind of facilities and open structure which only a few large colleges achieved up to the 1950s are now available in most.

It is equally remarkable, as Mr Hewett points out in chapter two that this expansion in size and numbers has gone on side by side with improvements in the quality of the work. During this same period of expansion, qualifications of both students and staff have risen steadily, the length of the normal course has been extended from two years to three so that greater depth of study has been possible, and most colleges now offer B.Ed. courses of four years' duration to a proportion of their students, the work for these courses being mainly or wholly undertaken by the college. More recently still, a good many colleges have added one-year postgraduate courses to their offerings while some are involved in the growing provision of B.Ed. courses for practising teachers whether by the local university or by the open university.

This is then in many respects a remarkable success story for which all concerned, the Department of Education and Science, the universities, the voluntary bodies and Local Education Authorities, and not least the colleges themselves, can rightly take credit. Why then the spate of criticism and the generally accepted need for enquiry? There are a number of possible connections between these two phenomena, some of them obvious enough. Success can rouse very mixed feelings in other people. Some of the critics seem to be complaining that Cinderella, now a princess, is not so good at scraping and scouring as once she was. At the same time she is obviously now owner of valuable real estate and subject to take-over bids and offers of alliance. Can she be detached from that university alliance she seems to have set her heart upon?

There is also the point, which has often been made throughout the period of expansion in both quantity and quality, that this was no time for a fundamental review of purpose and structure. In any case, everybody was too busy to undertake it. Furthermore, what the colleges needed most was room to breathe and expand in, a relaxation of the intense pressures and rigid boundaries of the traditional two-year course. For whatever reason, no fundamental review of purpose and structure was undertaken in this period and no doubt, in view of all the other changes going on in the colleges, it was just as well. For it is now abundantly clear that the last decade of expansion has brought the colleges to the threshold of a new stage in their development; the hard brown case of the chrysalis has split; what will emerge?

The transformation which has been going on within the hard case of the colleges in the direction of academic upgrading and increased depth of study has tended to sharpen the dichotomy which has existed since the 1920s between two aspects of the course, the main subject and education. Both are the products of evolution within the history of the colleges. The main subject reached its present form by a process of shrinkage, selection and concentration. In the early days of the colleges students studied subjects over the whole range of the elementary curriculum, and this occupied most of their time. The development of secondary (grammar) schools after 1902 gradually freed the colleges from this obligation, the number of subjects studied as such was reduced to one (or two); at the same time the reasons for study of the main subject were de-vocationalized. This had the advantage of creating a continuity of specialized study with the sixth forms of grammar schools from which the college students (and staff too) were mainly drawn. It also brought the college main course closer in both content and standards to the study of that subject in a university degree course. This undoubtedly eased the way for the universities' acceptance of the B.Ed. degree and now opens up further possibilities for the development of colleges as institutions which might make a contribution to higher education in general and not be so specifically geared, as has hitherto been the case, to the preparation of teachers. One of the main criticisms of Colleges of Education in recent years has been that they are 'monotechnic' institutions whose students have no freedom of vocational choice and little contact with students preparing for other professions. It is said that a good many college students today would welcome the possibility of deferring choice until near the end of their course as is the case with those entering the profession via an open-ended university course. It should be noted that this course also, until fairly recently, was for many a tied course in which a student pledged himself to teach in return for a grant which enabled him to accept a university place. It would seem that some relaxing of vocational bonds is now equally necessary for the colleges if they are to make the contribution to the expanding system of higher education of which they are obviously capable.

The other chief ingredient of the college course, the study and practice of education, reached its present position via a very different process of development from that of the main subject, though it was also one which in the end brought colleges and universities closer together. The process was one of expansion, exploration and colonization. The original ingredient in the nineteenth-century certificate course was very meagre indeed and closely linked to current practice: class and school management and methods of teaching the various subjects. From 1895 on, the syllabuses included references to the works of Bain and Sully, pioneers of the embryonic 'educational psychology' and to the work of Dr Arnold and Quick's *Educational Reformers*. Early in this century the syllabus headings changed from 'School Management' to 'Theory of Teaching' and later to the 'Principles of Education'. Thus, gradually, education became a recognized field of study though as yet its nature and structure as a subject were little explored. Undoubtedly the basis of it, between the first and second world wars, was provided by educational psychology, by then a recognized and expanding branch of psychology and, in its applications to selection and testing procedures, a minor industry. After the second world war, the older territories of psychology and history were expanded and consolidated and new territories added: notably in contributions to the study of education from what were themselves recently developed disciplines—sociology and analytic philosophy. The latter also produced a clearer definition of the nature of the subject education, as a field of study to which a number of different basic disciplines contribute and also one in which theory and practice are intimately linked.

The effect of all this has been the recognition, in recent years, of education as a proper field of university study from the undergraduate to the postgraduate and higher degree stages. At an International Conference on Education in 1884, R. H. Quick said, 'I say boldly that what English schoolmasters now stand in need of is *theory*; and, further, that the Universities have special advantages for meeting this need', and Professor Meiklejohn said, 'There is, in no University in England, a single person whose duty it is to guide a teacher in his daily practice. So far as the English Universities are concerned, Education is still in its amateur and empiric stage. Hence much friction, great waste of mental power, great waste of time and disappointing results.' What was envisaged by pioneers such as these has at last come near to realization. What the study of education in its modern form can provide is at any rate beginning to be something like the theoretical and research underpinning that the other professions have achieved (not so long ago in fact), and without which a profession cannot properly function. This leads me to two further observations which arise from this recognition of a professional base for education. One is that having built up at long last these close links between the theoretical and the practical, between the professional and the academic, the vocational and the liberal, it would be a pity to sever them by doing as some suggest and taking the universities out of the practical work field, or as others suggest, by taking the colleges out of the university orbit into some other

branch of higher education. The alliance of colleges and universities has been slowly forged and consolidated from the 1920s
onward. It is beginning to pay dividends. They have become
more like equal partners, covering between them the whole
range of teacher education. Many colleges today successfully
operate both graduate and postgraduate courses. Some university
departments are as interested in primary as in secondary work.
The university contribution to in-service education has been
considerable and ranges from conferences and short courses to
higher degree courses and research. Since the institution of the
B.Ed. the links between college and university departments, in
many subject fields have been forged and working relationships
established. University science departments have recently shown
special interest in the training of graduates in their subjects and
the Royal Society is acting as sponsor of their activities. My
second observation is that this development of the professional
studies side of the course opens up new possibilities for both
colleges and universities alike. When fully developed in its modern
form the study of education can be seen as (a) equally applicable
to those preparing for professions other than teaching, e.g. social
and personnel workers, and (b) a very suitable subject for inclusion
in a non-vocational course alongside other arts, science and social
science subjects. In fact a number of universities are now including
education as a first degree subject, some in a vocational context
(as at Keele for many years now), others in a non-vocational
context (as in Wales). At the same time this kind of development
obviously strengthens the case for widening the scope of the
degree work in colleges of education and including both vocational
and non-vocational courses, concurrent and consecutive.

A word about the plan of this book. The first two chapters
explore this question of a broader role for the colleges seen both
in terms of the historic development of institutions and in terms
of contemporary, economic and social pressures and needs. The
next four chapters take different aspects of the college course
beginning with a general consideration of the curricular structure
and passing on to the study of education, the main subject and
the organization of practical work. Chapter seven considers future
possibilities within the university, including both extensions of
work into the undergraduate years and extensions of the postgraduate courses themselves. Chapter eight takes a new look at the
field of in-service education, basing what is proposed on surveys

carried out for the N.F.E.R. The final chapter reviews the structure of teacher education, including both initial and in-service stages, and makes some radical proposals for a rephasing of the whole enterprise. Each contributor was given a free hand to develop his topic in his own way. The purpose of the book is twofold: to provide for those outside this particular field inside views on a number of important aspects of teacher education; and to provide both for those inside and those outside a basis for clarification of issues and the assessment of possibilities for the future.

One

Maurice Craft

**A Broader Role
for Colleges of
Education**

As other contributors to this volume observe, the 1960s witnessed
some of the most significant developments in the history of
English teacher education. The 1970s may see even greater
changes. The colleges may cease to be 'monotechnic' establishments concerned only with the professional education of teachers;
and, equally important, some may even move outside the sphere
of professional education altogether into a less narrowly specialized
role. Both these proposals are recurring themes in the current
discussion of the future of teacher education, and are part of the
general debate about the creation of a more co-ordinated and
flexible pattern of higher education.

This first chapter attempts a brief overview of the evolving
pattern of English teacher education, and falls into three parts:
first, a survey of the growth of the system and an assessment of
some significant determinants of change; second, a review of
proposals to unify higher education and to broaden the role of
the colleges; and third, a more detailed consideration of the
suggestions that we should now develop interprofessional and
liberal arts colleges.

The background

Teacher training in England originated in the 1840s, in early
industrialism. By 1845 there were twenty-two church training
colleges, and after the introduction of the pupil-teacher system
and the establishment of the Teacher's Certificate in 1846 the
pattern was virtually set for the rest of the century. Colleges were
small, residential, and rarely co-educational. They were State-
aided, inspected, and certificated, but were denominationally
controlled. Their regime was frugal and austere, a reflection
perhaps of the limited social function they were intended to serve
(to convey basic skills, and sobriety), and of the social role their
students would adopt (dedicated, but with a necessary social
distance). Their curricula, similarly, were severely functional; but
they also reflected some organizational characteristics (the un-
lettered enrolment, and the Oxbridge-educated principals and
Inspectorate), and so a liberal element was also included.

B

By the 1880s there were over forty training colleges, mainly
providing a two-year course. Compulsory elementary education
was, however, giving rise to an increased demand for teachers at
a time when the quality of the colleges' recruitment, their rigid
denominationalism and arid regime were becoming increasingly
out of step with the requirements of the times. Out of this interplay of social need and the lagging mechanism of teacher education
came the University Day Training Colleges, and their successors,
the U.D.E.s, and subsequent developments reinforced the
professional and educational divisions which were thus established.
After 1902, the new secondary schools drew heavily upon the
U.D.E.s. By 1913 there were eleven U.D.E.s offering the now
familiar one-year consecutive certificate course. The new L.E.A.
training colleges joined the voluntary colleges, outside the universities, in serving the great majority of the nation's children.
Twenty-two L.E.A. colleges were opened between 1904 and 1914,
almost doubling the number of training college places available.
Whether this dual system was the most functional response to
the diversifying economic and social structure of the time is a
somewhat academic question. It certainly offered some flexibility
and higher standards. Secondary education replaced the pupil-
teacher system as the main source of college recruitment; some of
the new L.E.A. colleges were non-residential and a few co-
educational, and most possessed much improved buildings and
amenities; but the U.D.E.s in particular, through their more
liberal regime and more rigorous curricula are thought to have
greatly influenced teacher education as a whole. The divisions
were, however, entrenched by the stagnation of the inter-war
years and have survived until the present.

In 1925, the Departmental Committee on the Training of
Teachers for Public Elementary Schools had recommended an
association between the universities and their local colleges, 'not
only with the object of interesting the universities more generally
in the training of teachers outside their precincts, but incidentally
as a means of giving the Training Colleges a greater measure of
autonomy' (Board of Education, 1925), and this led to the establishment of Joint Boards which gave the universities a co-ordinating
and examining role. But as the Board of Education still approved
syllabuses and examinations, and the Inspectorate sampled
students' practical teaching there was little real change, and the
value of the Joint Boards lay primarily in establishing the

basis of future co-operation between the universities and the colleges.

By 1938 there were over seventy training colleges, but this number had remained almost unchanged for nearly twenty years and student numbers had fallen considerably during this time. In 1944, the McNair Committee reviewed the recruitment and training of teachers and it too failed to unify the teaching body and its two avenues of professional training. Half the committee sought an integrated structure centred regionally on the universities, creating in each School of Education 'an organic federation of approved training institutions' (op. cit., para. 182); and half, fearing an unduly academic influence and not wishing to burden the universities with this numerically large responsibility, preferred college autonomy and development along existing lines. This latter, they felt, was the better scheme, involving 'an association of equals in the discharge of a common task instead of making the training colleges the dependants of the university' (para. 195). The outcome was a compromise which established our present pattern. The universities set up Institutes of Education to continue the co-ordinating role of the Joint Boards, each through an Area Training Organization which is governed by a Delegacy representing not only the university but also the colleges, the L.E.A.s, the central government, and the teachers. This was an advance on the earlier system, but each U.D.E. and each college retained its separate identity and form of government.

In 1963 the Robbins Committee published their comprehensive review of British higher education, placing teacher education into this broader context. By now there had been several major developments. The emergency training scheme of 1945–51, aimed at making good war shortages and providing for the raising of the school leaving age in 1947, had boosted teacher supply. In addition, seventeen new, permanent L.E.A. colleges were opened between 1946 and 1948, and student numbers rose from 13,000 in 1947 to 21,500 in 1950 and 24,000 in 1955 (Vaizey and Sheehan, 1968). By the 1950s the effect of the birthrate bulge of the immediate post-war years was appearing in the schools, combined with a 'trend' to staying on, and with the advent of the three-year course in 1960 the training colleges were becoming a very sizeable and important segment of British higher education. In 1900, teacher training had provided one-fifth of all students in higher education; in 1962 this had risen to nearly one-third (excluding advanced courses in Further Education) (Robbins Report, 1963, table 3). In 1963, there were 146 colleges in England and Wales compared with ninety in 1948, and student numbers had doubled since 1957 (Robbins Report, 1963; Taylor, 1969b).

Robbins' brief had been to review the nation's higher education system 'in the light of national needs and resources'. From the beginning the committee acknowledged that there *was* no system; that we had an independent (but publicly financed) university sector, and teacher education and further education sectors, both now engaged in advanced study. The 'system' had grown up piecemeal for a century, and had 'not been planned as a whole or developed within a framework consciously devised to promote harmonious development'. The committee felt that, 'however well the country may have been served by the largely unco-ordinated activities and initiatives of the past, we are clear that from now on these are not good enough'. As the Report puts it,

> higher education is so obviously and rightly of great public concern, and so large a proportion of its finance is provided in one way or another from the public purse, that it is difficult to defend the continued absence of co-ordinating principles and of a general conception of objectives. (*Op. cit.*, para. 19.)

Tight, centralized control was not envisaged, but rather a flexible system offering opportunity for growth and experiment; a rational system in which individual achievement would be freed from the ascriptive characteristics of particular institutions and where distinctions between institutions 'should be genuine, based on the nature of the work done and the organization appropriate to it', and not upon 'adventitious grounds, whether historical or social [which] are wholly alien to the spirit that should inform higher education'. In short, the committee recommended that 'there should be co-ordination, some principles of policy commonly accepted, some organization providing for rational allocation of scarce resources' (*op. cit.*, para. 39).

Robbins' recommendations for teacher education are now well known. Again, the establishment of university schools of education was proposed, incorporating the colleges as autonomous bodies financed through the universities, but again this failed. As in 1925, when the Joint Boards had been proposed, the L.E.A.s were unwilling to lose control of teacher supply (and, perhaps, of what had now become in many cases, large, prestigious colleges);

so was the government at a time of chronic teacher shortage and financial stringency. On the other hand, the training colleges henceforth became known as 'colleges of education'; secondly, Robbins' proposal for the establishment of a college-based B.Ed. degree has now come to pass; and thirdly, the L.E.A.s subsequently accepted a considerable liberalization of college government.[1] The colleges had gained in stature; but the final decisions probably reflected the history and organization of the educational system itself, rather than the national need for a more unified and less wasteful system of higher education. These internal divisions were further deepened in 1965 with the government's formal endorsement of a 'binary' policy, creating a clear separation between the 'autonomous' university sector and the 'public' sector embracing the colleges of education, a policy (paradoxically) designed to place 'a substantial part of the higher education system . . . under social control, directly responsible to social needs' (D.E.S., 1965).

Determinants of change

So much for a brief historical sketch. Teacher education in the 1960s found itself divided, and a partner in a fragmented tertiary system, partially within but largely outside the universities, and straddling the binary system. The arguments for a more co-ordinated and flexible pattern of higher education continue to be heard, and the future of teacher education and in particular the suggestions for a broader role for the colleges are very much part of this wider context.

Before going on to review the current proposals for change it might be worthwhile reflecting on the possible determinants of these past and present movements, for this may shed some light on our current enthusiasms. Some might argue that there is no discernible pattern, that teacher education is simply the product of the pragmatic reconciliation of need and response as interpreted by countless individuals and groups according to randomly changing material and ideological criteria. Alternatively, one might hypothesize a 'social process' view, i.e. that a social institution[2] (in this case formal education), comes into being to serve societal needs which can no longer be met by other social institutions (for example, the kinship group, the Church, or apprenticeship); that diversification and bureaucratization follow in due course (the development of teacher education, further education, higher education, and educational administration), giving rise to autonomous institutional characteristics, pressures, and interests; and that the subsequent development of an educational system may thus come to reflect both *societal* and *institutional* influences, the balance of pressures varying at different times.

According to this view, the beginnings of English teacher education might be said to have constituted a response to the urgent needs of early industrialism: literacy and social stability. With the diversification of the economy, the rise of a sizeable middle class, the entrenchment of the ethos of the early Victorian colleges, and the development of secondary education, teacher education came to reflect these societal and institutional forces through its two avenues, the colleges and the U.D.E.s. The inter-war stagnation of the economy was parallelled in teacher education, entrenching the internal divisions which both McNair and Robbins failed to bridge, and leading to the binary policy which might be thought of as an attempt to implement the talent-seeking and talent-developing needs of advanced industrialism through the mechanisms of an earlier age.

(a) *Institutional pressures*

These institutionally generated divisions are once again undergoing criticism and at a time when societal pressures (for reasons which are considered later) are mounting. However, it is perhaps somewhat paradoxical that the developments of the 1960s which have greatly strengthened teacher education (and, therefore, the *institutional* side of the equation) are now providing additional support for the *societal* arguments for integration in higher education. The colleges have become an important segment of tertiary education, well able to respond to continuing societal demands for expansion and anxious to do so.

The developments of the 1960s were themselves very largely a response to urgent societal demands.[3] A second birth-rate bulge (1956–64),[4] together with a continuing 'trend' to staying on and a sharp rise in the 'wastage' of young women teachers[5] precipitated a further crisis in teacher supply, and led in turn to another massive expansion of teacher education. Admissions more than doubled between 1960 and 1966 (D.E.S., 1968), total numbers in training almost trebled between 1960 and 1967 (D.E.S., 1969a) reaching 112,000 in 1969.[6] Colleges grew in size, and whereas in 1958 only three had more than 500 students, by 1962 this number had risen to 20 and by 1968 to 114, with 14 over 1,000 strong (Robbins Report, 1963, table 37; D.E.S., 1968). Equally important were the *qualitative* changes. The social composition of the colleges changed radically during the 1960s. One-third were co-educational in 1960, over 70 per cent in 1968. The qualifications of students, although still poorer than those of undergraduates, rose sharply (reflecting the 'trend'), and the proportion of 'mature' students admitted had reached around 20 per cent of the colleges' entry in 1968 (predominating in the new day colleges and college outposts) (D.E.S., 1968). The average age of staff had fallen sharply; and men staff came to outnumber women and are generally better qualified than women and more concerned about further study and research (Taylor, 1969a and b).

The ethos of the college system has changed with growth in scale (Shipman, 1965); with the rise in the proportion of L.E.A. (i.e. non-denominational) colleges from 44 per cent in 1948 to 68 per cent in 1968 (Taylor, 1969b); with the decline in residence (from 70 per cent in 1961 to 39 per cent in 1969) (D.E.S., 1968, 1970); and with governmental changes arising out of the Weaver Report (1966) and out of the operation of the B.Ed. degree. Finally, the 1960s witnessed major changes in college curricula: more differentiated studies pursued at greater depth in the new three-year and B.Ed. courses, and with greatly improved library, and other facilities; an expansion of in-service and advanced courses for practising teachers; and a sharp increase in the number of colleges admitting graduates to a P.G.C.E. course, an element which will continue to grow in the 1970s.[7]

(b) *Societal pressures*

The colleges of education thus emerge from the 1960s as a large, creative and influential sector of higher education, with the will and capacity to develop a broader role, and contributing an *institutional* thrust towards a more unified and flexible pattern of higher education which many observers are suggesting seems to be dictated by mounting *societal* pressures. These societal pressures are threefold: demographic, ideological, and economic. The *demographic* factor is basic and relatively straightforward. The 'bulge' of the 1940s found its way into higher education in the

1960s, producing a record number of eighteen-year-olds in 1966. But the bulge of the mid-50s will arrive in higher education from 1974 onwards and by 1980 the number of eighteen-year-olds may well be around 20 per cent higher than in 1970 (Table 1).

Table 1 *Number of eighteen-year-olds in England and Wales,* 1960–80

Year (1 Jan.)	Thousands	Year (1 Jan.)	Thousands	Year (1 Jan.)	Thousands
1960	539	1967	757	1974	660
1961	609	1968	716	1975	686
1962	643	1969	691	1976	710
1963	709*	1970	675	1977	728
1964	650	1971	669	1978	735
1965	771	1972	675	1979	769
1966	834	1973	668	1980	792

Source: D.E.S., 1969b, table 44. (Figures to 1968 from Registrar General; 1969–80 from Govt. Actuary's Dept.)
* Particularly affected by migration.

Demography, however, tells only half the story. An equally important contextual feature is *ideological*: the trend to staying on at school has continued unchecked, adding yearly to the numbers qualified to enter higher education. In 1955, 4·5 per cent of young people were achieving two or more 'A' level passes; by 1961 the figure was 6·9 per cent and by 1967 no less than 10·2 per cent (Table 2). In fact, despite fluctuations in the numbers of eighteen-year-olds in the population, the proportion qualified to enter higher education has risen consistently and in excess of Robbins' predictions. The 'trend' shows regional variations, however, and as the north gradually catches up with the south the 'trend' will become more marked.

The third contextual feature is *economic*, and there are two aspects to this. First, there is real concern about the soaring costs of education, and particularly of higher education, which reflect not only demographic and ideological changes but also the far higher cost per student compared with that in schools. Expenditure on universities, for example, has trebled since 1960 and doubled since 1963, compared with corresponding increases of 89 per cent and 52 per cent for schools (D.E.S., 1969c). As Layard *et al.* have put it, 'apart from electronics and natural gas, higher education has grown faster than any major national enterprise in the 1960s.' The *overall*, national cost of education was more than £2,200 millions in 1969, exceeding that on defence (D.E.S., 1970). This was over 6 per cent of the gross national product, compared with

Table 2 *Numbers and percentage of eighteen-year-olds in England and Wales obtaining two or more 'A' levels, 1960–80*

Year	Thousands	Age group obtaining 2 or more 'A' levels %	Year	Thousands	Age group obtaining 2 or more 'A' levels %
1960	38·1	6·6	1971	80·2	12·3
1961	43·3	6·9	1972	83·2	12·7
1962	50·8	7·6	1973	86·4	13·2
1963	53·3	8·0	1974	89·6	13·7
1964	60·6	8·3	1975	94·9	14·2
1965	73·2	9·2	1976	101·9	14·6
1966	75·4	9·6	1977	108·5	15·1
1967	79·0	10·2	1978	115·0	15·7
1968	77·8	10·7	1979	123·0	16·2
1969	77·5	11·3	1980	131·6	16·7
1970	78·3	11·8			

Source: Layard *et al.*, 1969. (Figures from 1966 are D.E.S. projections.)

2·5 per cent between the wars, and 3·2 per cent in the mid-50s (D.E.S., 1970; Vaizey and Sheehan, 1968), and the annual rate of growth in public spending on education has been running at a level at least three times higher than growth in G.N.P. in recent years (Maclure, 1968). There were, for example, over 377,000 teachers in England and Wales in February 1969, an increase of nearly 4 per cent on the previous year and of nearly 17 per cent in the previous five years (D.E.S., 1970).

This, however, brings us to a second and more basic aspect of the economic context, for it might be argued that this high level of expenditure on education (and especially on higher education) is quite appropriate for an advanced industrial society and is likely to continue. Employment in agriculture, forestry, fishing, mining and quarrying (i.e. the primary sector) is falling rapidly, while that in manufacturing and in service occupations (the secondary and tertiary sectors) is rising. Within the secondary sector there is a continuing fall in unskilled employment and a contraction of such long established industries as textiles; but the skilled trades and particularly such newer science-based industries as engineering, plastics and chemicals are expanding. Employment in electronics, for example, increased by 25 per cent between 1951 and 1961, and that in plastics more than doubled. Most spectacular of all has been the continued growth of *service* occupations—distribution, banking, the professions—and of administrative, clerical and technical workers in industry (Marsh, 1965; Central Statistical Office, 1969). In short, there is an accelerating demand for skill, and in general, the more advanced the skill the greater the demand.

No doubt these demographic, ideological and economic factors are interrelated: growth of G.N.P. may have influenced patterns of marriage and family-building in the mid-50s, and (together with the continuing democratization of British society) educational and occupational aspirations also. The combined 'bulges' and trend have inflated education costs, and long-term occupational changes promise no relaxation of this upward course of expenditure: the demand for advanced technical and professional qualifications from the manufacturing and service sectors is certain to accelerate; secondly, the continued rise of *women's* white-collar and professional employment may well have a profound influence on the aspirational levels of future generations;[8] and thirdly, the trend to large-scale capital-intensive industry and the 'affluent worker' may also be expected to enhance levels of aspiration (Goldthorpe *et al.*, 1969; Toomey, 1969).

Proposals for a unitary system

So far this chapter has surveyed the growth of English teacher education, and has argued that in responding to pressing societal needs the colleges of education have developed the capacity to make a larger and more flexible contribution to an expansion of higher education which seems inevitable, given the demographic, ideological and economic imperatives which have been outlined. A second task is to consider some of the proposals for a more unified tertiary system into which the reformed colleges would fit.

Faced with the prospect of a steadily rising demand for higher education it is not surprising that Robbins' 'guiding principles' should be recurring themes in contemporary discussions: education as an essential means of economic growth, education for the enrichment of all who can profit by it, and a rational, co-ordinated, flexible system which maximizes scarce resources (*op. cit.*, chap. 2). There is much talk of increasing productivity in higher education: more intensive use of buildings and equipment, more efficient teaching and a greater use of educational technology, student loans instead of grants, changes in the staff-student ratio, and so on. But these are the tactics of marginal change. More far-reaching strategies have also been proposed, and a number were submitted in evidence to the *Parliamentary Select Committee on Education and Science* which was appointed in 1969 to examine teacher training.

Most observers have attacked the binary system as fostering unnecessary status distinctions and a maldistribution of scarce resources, and arguing for a more unified pattern. One of the most far-reaching suggestions is that of Professor Pedley (1969) which has proposed a unified regional structure, the 'comprehensive university', incorporating teacher education and all other branches of further and higher education. Professor Pedley claims that

> Such a pattern would help to sweep out the cobwebs from
> universities which are too isolated in their thinking, and also
> to remove the feeling of inferiority which dogs the colleges.
> It would, moreover, help to promote that equal respect for
> post-school education at all levels, including part-time as
> well as full-time education, and that freedom of movement
> from one type of course to another, which a democratic
> society might be expected to desire.

This seminal paper which does not always distinguish functional specialization from wasteful duplication, and which may under-estimate the deep-rooted loyalties of a long-fragmented system, nonetheless accurately reflects profound societal trends and its central notions have been echoed in turn by young teachers (N.U.T., 1969), the N.U.T. (1970), the N.U.S.,[9] and others. The N.U.T. criticized the wasteful duplication of buildings and equipment and the uneconomic use of manpower, and urged the need to plan higher education as a whole.

The colleges of education and the technical colleges cannot plan their courses to the greatest advantage if the university sector of higher education is free to develop its courses irrespective of what is being done elsewhere; nor can the total output of students from higher education bear any relation to employment prospects while the three sectors, university, teacher training and further education, are uncoordinated and have no regard to national need.

The N.U.S. endorsed this, while at the same time stressing the value of 'creating a new awareness of each sector as a national entity with its own distinctive and vital functions and its own educational autonomy within the national system. This is important if the comprehensive university is to be seen as a partnership, not as a "take-over" ' —a clear reminder of Robbins' views on autonomy within a planned system. The voluntary colleges of education have similarly advocated 'an open, but unitary, pattern of higher education';[10] and the N.A.S. felt that teacher education 'should become part of the general higher education establishment'.[11]

Federalism is therefore the means which has been most often proposed. For the A.T.C.D.E. (1970), concerned more specifically with provision for teacher education, this would be a development of the present A.T.O., whereby 'colleges could be grouped within a federated structure and associated with a parent university which would be responsible for overseeing, developing and validating courses and awards', much as the present Institutes of Education now function but with wider responsibilities. On a wider front, a Fabian group (1970) has advocated regional federalisms embracing all eighteen-plus education, centrally planned and co-ordinated but providing for diversity and flexibility. The 'comprehensive university', they felt, seems to imply an end to separation and selection in tertiary education; but this would mean gigantic universities in which the separate components 'would cease to have much common identity', and denies the reality of specialization of interests among eighteen-year-olds.

Eric Robinson's strictures were harsher. In reviewing the anti-binary feelings of the late 1960s which questioned the paradox of comprehensive secondary education followed by segregated higher education, Robinson (1968) claims that 'the fallacy of this analogy with comprehensive secondary reform is gross and easily exposed. . . . Comprehensive secondary education embraces all children in the secondary school range. Unitary higher education would embrace only an elite minority of the young people in the relevant age range, for "higher education" is only a minor part of the whole of post-school ("tertiary") education.' This means that 'The unification of the education of professionals—teachers, engineers, doctors, lawyers and so on—would be secured at the cost of the virtually complete segregation of their education from the education of sub-professionals and non-professionals—clerks, technicians, shopkeepers and plumbers.' All the latter would remain in 'further' and 'adult' education. So for Robinson, a unified system of eighteen-plus education centred on the universities is no improvement on a binary system offering two avenues of eighteen-plus education. A far more extensive rationalization of 'tertiary' (i.e. fifteen-plus) education is required.

The L.E.A.s have opposed these kinds of ideas. Dr Ollerenshaw, representing the Association of Municipal Corporations, for example, has argued that the L.E.A.s should continue to have an effective voice in the training of teachers, and in the government of colleges of education, for 'we are the direct customers; we have the incentive and motivation; we want the teachers in our schools.'[12] This manpower-orientated view seems very clearly to reflect institutional rather than societal considerations, and Sir William Alexander, representing the Association of Education Committees, seems at first sight to be drawing an important distinction in separating the 'education' of teachers (which he feels is properly a university function) from their 'training' (a function of professional and employing bodies).[13] This at least accepts that teaching involves more than technique. But it fails to recognize that education embodies several fundamental social processes (socialization, social control, which are discussed later), and executes numerous vital social functions (the development and allocation of skill, for example), so that teachers are ultimately legitimized by and are responsible to *society*, and not professional associations or employing bodies. Furthermore, the effective integration of theory and practice is currently a major objective of teacher education; to seek a clearer separation would be dysfunctional.

The universities have also reflected a degree of institutional inertia and have been cautious in their reactions to proposals for the unification of higher education. The Committee of Vice-Chancellors (1970) has rightly pointed out the distinctive roles of

the several segments of higher education, but has perhaps over-
stated their complementary nature and understated the overlaps
of function and provision. The committee has, however, given
much thought to productivity and to the economy of resources,
including the sharing of facilities with other, non-university bodies,
and is properly concerned with the maintenance of high academic
standards in a period of expansion and rapid change. The A.U.T.
(1970) goes a little further in declaring the binary system 'an
unnatural creation born of financial illusions', and arguing that
higher education is a 'unitary system' in its objectives, i.e.
'developing to their full potential as large a proportion of the
population as has the necessary ability'. Their policy statement
'welcomes co-operation between universities and other institutions
of higher education on a growing scale' (particularly between
universities and colleges of education); it advocates a common
admissions system and easier transferability between courses, a
rationalization of resources, and a rather broader role for the
U.G.C. which might consider channelling funds also to polytechnics and colleges of education and perhaps adopting 'an
advisory role with respect to the whole field of higher education'.

For some university opinion, a rationalization of higher education cannot be separated from greater central government control
and this, it is thought, might endanger academic freedom which
is, essentially, the need to ensure the unlimited growth and refinement of knowledge, a vital social function in an advanced society
and one professing liberal ideals. On the other hand, the very
importance of this social function (and its financial costs) naturally
attract government concern. For Pierson[14] a guarantee of academic
freedom in a more unified system could be provided by the use of
earmarked grants. Pierson argues that

> there is no logical argument for universities, polytechnics,
> and colleges of education to be financed through different
> channels or on different principles. The differences should
> lie in the relative proportions of earmarked and non-earmarked
> grant. Universities must have a large proportion of non-
> earmarked grant to maintain their self-motivated research
> programmes. Polytechnics and colleges of education, which
> will be primarily teaching institutions, may have a smaller
> proportion of non-earmarked grant; but they must have
> some.

A new role for the colleges of education

Of these various proposals, a number have sketched a new role for the Colleges of Education within a unified system, in which delayed career choice and an end to the academic isolation of student teachers are basic features. The former usually implies an increased liberal element, while the latter, involving the admission of trainees for other professions implies the reverse, a *multi*-vocational (rather than 'monotechnic') bias. The N.U.T. young teachers' report (*op. cit.*), for example, recommends that students at eighteen-plus might enrol for a one-and-a-half to two-year 'social studies' course in a common 'campus' setting, to be followed by a year in the field as a paid ancillary worker in teaching or social work, and then by a further one-and-a-half to two years in teacher education or some other specialization. This scheme, despite the 'campus' setting among other types of college, would however still leave the colleges of education as specialist establishments, although it clearly allows for delayed vocational choice, or for a 'terminal' period of non-vocational tertiary education. The second N.U.T. report (*op. cit.*) goes rather further and advocates an end to 'mono-faculty' colleges and the admission of students pursuing qualifications in social welfare, as well as those who are uncertain about teaching and wish to leave a decision until the fourth year when they could take an 'end-on' P.G.C.E. Many students would still follow the present concurrent course, but for four years, and this might eventually lead to a graduate qualification. The report recommends that colleges should be grouped within Robbins-style schools of education, and that they should also develop close working relations with further education. The N.U.S. (*op. cit.*) similarly recommended that colleges should offer 'a spread of courses, both academic and professional, related to the social services, to education, and to child care', and they made the point often made in the past that interprofessional colleges might ease inter-occupational career mobility.

Variations on the same themes have been put forward by Goldsmiths College, London (Chesterman and Pinker),[15] by Professor Rée (1970), and by the Vice-Chancellor of Lancaster University (Carter, 1970). Chesterman recommends that A.T.O.s 'should have their scope widened to include a big variety of community services, e.g. youth service, community workers, child care workers, probation officers, art and occupational therapists, etc.', with courses of common length and the possibility of transfer during training. Colleges would offer a two-year general course, delaying vocational choice until the third year and awarding a pass degree after successful completion of a probationary year in the field. Pinker and Carter have similarly questioned the segregated training of teachers (and also of nurses and lawyers) and their early vocational commitment, and Carter and Bullock (1970) have advocated the establishment of degree-awarding liberal arts colleges based in some cases on colleges of education and further education. Porter[16] has specifically proposed the establishment of a three-year liberal arts programme at the Berkshire College of Education leading to a first degree, which might then be followed by a P.G.C.E. or other professional training also offered by the College. The present three-year concurrent and four-year B.Ed. courses would remain. The 'liberal arts' degree would include three elements: education (involving fieldwork in school or community), a main subject, and a liberal arts option. This is one of the first such schemes to be outlined in any detail; as Porter explains,

> The liberal arts option should stress the relationship between areas of knowledge and introduce the student to new experiences particularly in the creative arts and sciences. The courses should have a large element of choice for the student and thus it appears inevitable that some form of credit system should be introduced. Throughout the course counselling and guidance of students towards appropriate occupational outlets would be most important. The co-operation of other institutions of higher and further education would also be of prime importance.

Clearly, many colleges of education now possess the nucleus of skills, facilities and experience to develop liberal arts programmes up to general degree standard, for many now contribute some or all the courses comprising a B.Ed. degree. Some of the larger colleges could offer a wide curriculum, while others could probably organize joint programmes in association with neighbouring colleges in their A.T.O. A number (and not only the specialist colleges) have developed particular strengths, for example in social science or rural science, and might offer courses related to these areas. On the other hand, a substantial minority for reasons of size or geographical isolation might find it difficult to develop viable liberal arts programmes and a status hierarchy of colleges would quickly develop. Although it is probably true that such a hierarchy now exists the ending of the 'monotechnic' college would put the seal on it.

Staffing need not be the problem that some observers feel it would be. While Taylor (1969b) has demonstrated the disparity in academic qualifications between colleges and universities over-all, if a new staff role is created which legitimizes academic research (and if time and facilities are made available for this), the gap could be narrowed. More than this it can be argued that such a change of role is essential if liberal arts teaching is to be of the first order, and the heavy teaching/administrative loads of college staff would have to be substantially reduced. Would college governors and college staffs be willing to make such a fundamental change? More important perhaps, would it be possible to combine in a single organization the value-trans-mission function of professional socialization and the more academic role commitments of a university department? Up to a point this dichotomy now exists between college education and main subject departments and is a source of stress. Or would change be more feasible if some colleges were to become liberal arts only, while others offered several (compatible) vocational trainings and became interprofessional colleges? These are issues which need to be clarified.

How do the universities view these kinds of proposals? The attitude of the Committee of Vice-Chancellors (*op. cit.*) is not at all discouraging. They envisage the possibility of 'some specific enlargement of the role of the colleges beyond that of the training of teachers . . . certain areas of study—perhaps in aspects of social work or in parts of the liberal arts field . . . could well be associated effectively with the traditional activities of the colleges of educa-tion and could serve not only as a valuable supplement to existing facilities but also as a stimulus to those undergoing teacher training'. But their proposal that a 'two-year initial course' might be based in the colleges of education or in liberal arts type colleges, from which promising students might then proceed to universities for further study seems to underestimate the capacity of those colleges already deeply involved in B.Ed. work. The A.U.T. (*op. cit.*) is more positive:

C

To help meet the demand for places, to help cope with the
apparently growing need for certain qualifications, and to make
full use of the facilities and special skills of the colleges of
education [the A.U.T]. would be pleased to see them, in
appropriate cases, expand into allied social and administrative
fields with openings, as in the B.Ed., for entrants to proceed
to degree-level work.

Professor Ross[17] sees it all very differently: a graduate profession
trained largely in the universities and polytechnics, with the
colleges of education absorbed as additional university accommodation or employed as centres of in-service training and
research. This seems a very long way ahead given the present
institutional pressures. The A.T.C.D.E. plan on the other hand
seems to offer a realistic blend of the essential elements of all the
others, without departing too radically from what might be
thought of as a logical line of development. The colleges, the paper
suggests, could establish 'broadly based courses in the sciences,
the humanities, the creative arts, and social and behavioural
studies, which would permit a considerable element of inter-
disciplinary study'. These would be degree courses in their own
right, but could be followed by P.G.C.E. or other professional
training. The present Certificate/B.Ed. structure would continue,
but an all-graduate profession is the long-term aim. This variety
of courses would thus offer considerable flexibility by providing
easy transfer and delayed vocational choice for those who wish it
(provided, of course, that the organizational strains of a multi-
purpose college which were discussed earlier could be contained),
and is illustrated in Table 3.
     So far as college government is concerned, the paper argues that,
'The principle of federated groups of colleges in association with a
parent university would have many of the advantages claimed by
the advocates of comprehensive higher education and/or "poly-
universities" without most of the attendant disadvantages.' It
would facilitate decentralized university expansion and the
establishment of university outposts for adult education, and
would end the academic isolation of student teachers.[18]

Rationale for change

This chapter has sought to review the origins and growth of the
colleges of education, to outline the contemporary reassessment of

Table 3 *A possible structure of college courses*

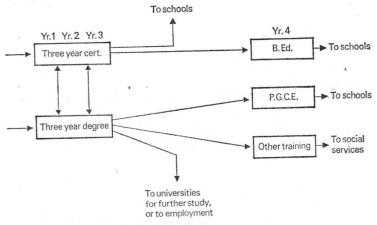

Source: A.T.C.D.E., *op. cit.*, Appendix 2.

their role, and to place this reassessment in the context of wider proposals for change in higher education. It has also hypothesized that the interplay of institutional and societal forces may help to explain change; but this is doubtless a considerable over-simplification and in fact tells us little of the *mechanisms* of change. The political and social traditions of decentralization, gradualism, and pragmatism may take us a little further and help to account, say, for the slowness and piecemeal nature of change in education; but this is still insufficient. How, for example, is the outpouring of opinion on teacher education in the late 1960s to be explained? No doubt many of the policy statements were associated with the former government's appointment of a Parliamentary Select Committee to examine teacher training, and its setting up of the regional A.T.O. enquiries. But what precipitated these government decisions? Vigorous institutional vested interests and compelling societal pressures, mediated through pragmatic gradualism.

Similarly, much patient research would be needed to account for tactical preferences within broad strategies of change, to explain, for example, the relative unpopularity of the liberal arts idea in this country compared with a continuing interest in interprofessionalism. The Robbins Committee (*op. cit.*) considered the establishment of liberal arts colleges, but preferred to see developments within the colleges of education or regional colleges

of further education rather than the establishment of a new kind
of organization:

> We think it better in general to encourage innovations in
> established institutions than to attempt to begin, with
> restricted aspirations, on a completely new basis. Liberal arts
> colleges founded specifically to deal with work of a limited
> range would have difficulty in establishing a reputation. They
> would not be building on the long experience gained in
> further education and in the education of teachers, nor would
> they have the attraction for staff and students of a university
> proper.

The committee similarly rejected the creation of separate junior
or preparatory colleges to undertake advanced sixth form and
first year university work, and recommended that 'the needs of
the future should be met by developing present types of institution'. This was consistent with the committee's concern to restrict
the fragmentation of higher education to what is functionally
necessary and to avoid needless, irrational divisions.

The proposal that colleges of education admit social workers
of various kinds, on the other hand, has more diverse roots and
has become a progressively more popular idea on both pragmatic
and theoretical grounds, so that recent years have seen growing
experimentation and blurring of professional boundaries (Craft,
1970b). The former Secretary of State, Mr Edward Short. had
declared his dislike of the 'monotechnic' college of education,[19]
and a former Minister of State, Mrs Shirley Williams, had
similarly expressed interest in interprofessional experiments,
'. . . a development we are anxious to encourage'.[20] More recently,
Mrs Margaret Thatcher has expressed precisely the same senti-
ments.[21] Most of the major post-war reports on education have
advocated a broadening of the colleges' role in this particular
direction.[22] Plowden (1967) had criticized the early choice of
career forced upon college students and their segregation in
training, and like Robbins (*op. cit.*),[23] Newsom (1963) and McNair
(1944) had recommended further experiment in the joint training
of teachers and social workers. Albemarle (1965) had also
expressed interest in the possible gains to be derived from common
core courses in the joint training of youth employment officers,
teachers, youth leaders, social caseworkers, and personnel

managers; while Albemarle (1960) had commented upon the common recruitment of youth work, teaching and social work, and upon the desirability of easier transfer (for youth workers) to 'other professional work in education or the social services'— something which has come closer since the implementation of D.E.S. Circular 3/70 and the establishment of four two-year courses in youth and community work. Indeed, the recurring themes of common sources of recruitment, the desirability of delayed vocational choice and easier transfer from one professional avenue to another in training, closer collaboration in the field between professionals who have trained together, and easier transfer from one professional role to another can be found in numerous reports in recent years.[24]

Theoretical roots of interprofessionalism

Many of these recommendations were probably motivated by a variety of pragmatic considerations. But it might be argued that there are also theoretical justifications for experimenting with interprofessional training, and this may account for the increasing popularity of the interprofessional idea in recent years. In this final section this more theoretical perspective is briefly considered.

There are several strands of interprofessional thinking. One suggests that there is a *mental health* component in teaching and that to some extent the teacher is unavoidably a therapist. Another veers more to a *social process* view and considers that teachers and social workers share overlapping social functions. The compensatory education movement falls between the two: those of its exponents who stress 'social education' and the use of social group work as a central technique in both formal and informal education tend to be associated with the mental health view of interprofessionalism; those who are firmly curriculum-orientated tend to be interprofessionally relatively neutral; and those who focus on school welfare techniques (counselling, parent-teacher relations, community development) may have both a mental health and a social process commitment. But there are, of course, no hard and fast dividing lines in this polarization of views.

On the mental health side Professor Halmos (1959), a pioneer of the interprofessional idea, has argued that the concepts of teaching and therapy are not easily separated: that teaching (the conveying of information and skills) has a modifying influence on

personality, while therapy has a considerable influence on understanding (knowledge) as well as on the effectiveness of skills.
Taken to an extreme this might be thought to legitimize amateur
psychotherapy in the classroom, something which few would feel
desirable, and this has been strongly criticized by Bantock (1967)
and others. On the other hand, a mechanistic view of learning
which takes no account of motivation in the interaction system
of the classroom can hardly be complete. As a macro-social
process view, I have argued elsewhere that teachers and social
workers might be thought to share 'overlapping perspectives',
that both are centrally concerned with *socialization* for example;
that teachers and social workers might be placed at different
points on a socialization continuum according to the ameliorative
loading of their respective roles—for there are many different
kinds of teacher and social worker; that such basic principles of
social work as acceptance or self-determination apply also to
teaching, but similarly along a continuum; that diffuseness of role
applies to both, again, along a continuum; and that these continua
can then be found to demonstrate much occupational overlap
(Craft, 1967, 1969; Bulman *et al.*, 1970).

As the sociological theorist Talcott Parsons puts it (1951),
socialization is a fundamental social process by which individuals
internalize not only generalized character traits (adaptiveness, say)
but also more specific role orientations (sex roles, for example).
Without this process no social system would cohere and survive.
Teachers may thus be placed at one end of a socialization continuum and social workers at the other, the former being concerned
with laying *foundations* of belief and action (i.e. with 'apprenticeship') and the latter with *maladjustments* of belief and action (i.e.
with 'alleviation'). As Professor Tibble has written (1959), both
teachers and social workers 'are essentially engaged in bringing
about changes of one kind or another in people, adults or children,
who are by definition in a state of need: either because of their
immaturity and dependence as children or because of some
maladjustment between person and environment'. Elsewhere
(1967) he argues that,

> in both cases something has to be learned—knowledge, skill,
> attitudes—which is relevant to the need. The difference can
> perhaps most profitably be thought of in terms of education
> and re-education, since the social worker is more likely to be

specifically involved in repairing defects of knowledge, changing unsatisfactory attitudes, relearning of social skills and so on.

Education and re-education is one way of viewing the two ends of the continuum, but I would prefer socialization and re-socialization, for the latter introduces a further theoretical perspective which is central to this discussion. Parsons (*op. cit.*) suggests that a second major process by which a society seeks to maintain equilibrium is that of *social control*, the means by which deviant behaviour which threatens to become seriously disruptive is re-channelled, insulated, or 're-integrated'. As Parsons notes, there is no clear dividing line between the processes of socialization and social control, the one depending on the success of the other, a fact which is suggested in Table 4.

Table 4   *Socialization and social control*

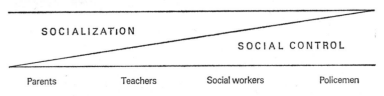

Using this simple model one may hypothesize that it is the centre part of the continuum that is most relevant to the analysis of interprofessionalism (Table 5).

Table 5   *Interprofessionalism, socialization and social control*

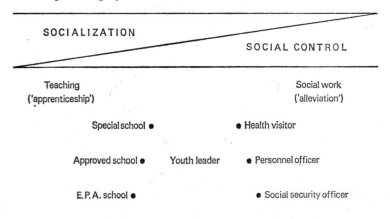

Here the continuum indicates that in general the element of social control increases with the welfare (or 'alleviative') loading of the professional role, i.e. as one moves from teaching to social work. The *intra*-professional variations are important for these indicate the areas of overlap between teaching and social work: some teachers are largely concerned with the educationally or socially deviant (teachers in E.P.A., approved, or special schools, for example), while some social workers are largely concerned with the 'normal' and have relatively 'instrumental' roles concerned more with the provision of technical advice or material help than with therapy. Youth workers generally have *both* types of function in a group or community setting, but one or the other will predominate depending on the particular appointment, a point which is taken up later.

The notions of acceptance and self-determination might also be placed on a continuum where maximum latitude is allowed by, say, parents and minimum latitude by, say, prison warders; here again teaching and social work would fall between these two extremes (Table 6).

Table 6 *Acceptance and self-determination*

Maximal	Minimal	Maximal	Minimal
Homes	Schools	Social Work Agencies	Prisons

Here the continuum is bi-modal, reflecting the organizational characteristics of schools and welfare agencies: schools are concerned with children and in large numbers, while the social worker's clients are normally adults and are faced on a one-to-one basis, hence the greater *authority* loading of the teacher's role (Gibbs, 1959; Meyer *et al.*, 1968). But the differences are matters of technique, the objectives (socialization and social control), as suggested in Table 1, overlap. The centre section of the continuum when extracted and considered in more detail again suggests major overlaps of perspective and principle within the two professional roles (Table 7).

The traditional grammar school might accept few deviations from

Table 7 *Interprofessionalism, acceptance and self-determination*

Teaching				Social Work
Minimal				*Maximal*
Grammar school	Infant school	Youth Leader	Family casework	Psychotherapy

the school's established codes of conduct, while for the psycho-therapist no expressed attitudes would be unacceptable. The traditional grammar school might utilize a rigid curriculum allowing little self-determination in learning procedures compared with the far greater flexibility in social casework. But these are extreme cases which are used to illustrate the overlaps of inter-mediate roles. Primary school teachers might be closer to the social work model (Musgrove and Taylor, 1969; Blyth, 1967), and some caseworkers may make considerable use of authority (Foren and Bailey, 1968).

Once again it is suggested that these are differences in *technique* and not in objectives. The social work notions of acceptance and self-determination are not open-ended, as several social work theorists have clearly stated. Hollis (1940) for example, writes that 'it is important that the client's right to self-determination exists until it is demonstrated that the exercise of this right would be highly detrimental to himself and to others'; while Biestek (1961) says that 'the client's right to self-determination, however, is limited by the client's capacity for positive and constructive decision making, by the framework of civil and moral law, and by the function of the agency'. This kind of qualification undermines any suggestion that these principles are individual 'rights' (Plant, 1970), but supports the notion that (like teachers) social workers are legitimized by society as agents of social control (Leonard, 1965; Nursten, 1965); psychotherapy, in fact, might be regarded as a classic case of such an agency (Parsons, 1951). As Taylor (1958) has written:

> Caseworkers are the agents of the agency—and therefore of the community—in their treatment relationships with clients. As agents of the community, caseworkers become part of the process by which society seeks to secure a measure of

conformity to expectations and, in this sense, casework has
a social control function.[25]

Finally, Parsons' scheme of 'pattern variables' (*op. cit.*) offers
a further means of illustrating overlaps in the roles of teacher and
social worker. Take, for example,t he dimension of diffuseness *v.*
specificity (Table 8).

Table 8   *Role diffuseness*

Maximal	Minimal	Maximal	Minimal
Parents	Teachers	Social Workers	Policemen

For parents the role demands are almost endless—they are the
source of love, discipline, food, shelter, good times; but the role
of the policeman is far more circumscribed and specific. Between
the two extremes fall the roles of teacher and social worker
(Table 9).

Table 9   *Interprofessionalism and role diffuseness*

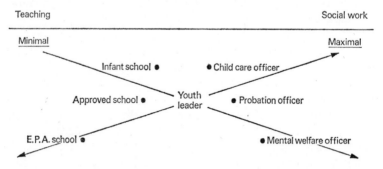

Here the most 'traditional' schools would subscribe to relatively
clear-cut aims and methods (academic success through rigid
streaming, say), using relatively clear-cut measure of achievement
(external examinations, for example), and the teacher's role in
such schools would be relatively specific. At the other end of the
continuum, in psychotherapy, say, aims and methods would be

far more ill-defined and achievement would be almost impossible to measure precisely.[26] Once again, these are hypothetical extremes and the intermediate role positions illustrate the huge area of overlap; for the roles of both teachers and social workers (notwithstanding a *range* of diffuseness within each profession, and a polarization at each end of the continuum), are essentially diffuse in nature (Wilson, 1962; Leonard, 1966; Nokes, 1967). Each profession lacks such clearly recognizable and obviously indispensable techniques and insights as are possessed by the pilot or the surgeon; and no one can be certain what knowledge, skills and attitudes are 'essential' for the practising teacher or social worker (Timms, 1968).

The future

This chapter has attempted to review the changing structure of teacher education, and to assess some of the determinants of change, within the broader context of British higher education. In particular, it has considered contemporary proposals for a wider role for the colleges of education which might now become part of the more general provision of tertiary education, or which might embrace a wider range of professional trainings. It has been argued that both developments would be in the line with the needs of a complex, industrial society on a variety of grounds; but what are the possibilities, for, societal needs apart, institutional interests are now running in several directions? The colleges of education would clearly welcome a broader role, and with such a range of colleges some diversification should not be impossible given the goodwill of the several elements of college government. But despite the central government's expressed interest in ending their 'monotechnic' status and the possibility that some universities might welcome a new relationship with the colleges, the attitude of the L.E.A.s is not yet clear. Of equal importance is the attitude of further education: how do the polytechnics and colleges of F.E. feel about the possible loss of these advanced courses? Will teacher education be willing to accept a merging of functions with further education as part of a re-organization? There are also complicated problems of academic and professional legitimacy arising out of the numerous university, professional and governmental bodies concerned in any proposal to coordinate the training of teachers and social workers.

Of one thing we may be reasonably sure, there is unlikely to be
any grand plan. If change comes about it will be more likely to
emerge from local, pragmatic advance on the basis of favourable
local conditions, and the regional A.T.O. enquiries now underway
may be a significant factor in this. The danger is likely to be
'centrifugalism', as it is in secondary education. The much-
needed flexibility in higher education can gain much from local
initiatives; but is it too late—or perhaps too soon—to reassess
the national framework? Let us hope not.

Notes

1 The Weaver Report (1966), implemented by the government in
   1967.
2 In the sociological sense, i.e. not an organization, but a set of
   interrelated norms centred about a fundamental human problem.
3 But not entirely: the case for a three-year Teacher's Certificate
   course, for example, has been argued by teachers and teacher
   trainers for a long time, and was recommended by the McNair
   Committee (1944) and, fifty years earlier, by the Cross Commission
   (1888).
4 Births in 1964 were 31·7 per cent higher than in 1955 (Kelsall,
   1970).
5 Marriage rates per thousand of the population have risen steadily
   during this century and this trend has been combined more
   recently with a trend to earlier marriage and earlier family-building.
   (Kelsall, 1970; Central Statistical Office, 1969.)
6 This was almost one-half the total number of university students
   in 1969, compared with one-quarter in 1900 and one-third in 1954.
   (Robbins Report, 1963, table 3; D.E.S., 1970.)
7 The number doubled between 1967 and 1969 (D.E.S., 1970).
8 Much literature in the sociology of education has commented on
   the connection between a mother's white-collar occupation before
   marriage and subsequent patterns of motivation and achievement
   in her children (Craft, 1970a).
9 Select Committee on Education and Science (1970), 30, vi.
10 Ibid., 30, iv.
11 Ibid., 30, v.
12 Select Committee on Education and Science (1969), 30, iii.
13 Select Committee on Education and Science (1970), 30, iv, and
   also Alexander (1969).
14 Select Committee on Education and Science (1970), 30, xii.
15 Ibid., 135, iv.
16 Ibid., 151, iv.
17 Ibid., 30, viii.
18 For fuller details see chapter 2.
19 Reported in the *Guardian*, 9 April 1970, p. 5.

20 Reported in *Hansard*, 23 July 1969, col. 1980.
21 Reported in *The Teacher*, 28 August 1970, p. 1.
22 Discussed in Bulman *et. al.*, chapter 11.
23 This was an important recommendation (para. 313), reflecting, perhaps, the evidence submitted not only by the A.T.C.D.E. but also the Association of Chief Education Officers and the Conference of Institute Directors.
24 For example D.E.S. (1969d), Gulbenkian Foundation (1968), Scottish Education Dept. (1968), D.E.S. (1955); but not, perhaps surprisingly, the Seebohm Report (1968) or the Morison Report (1962).
25 Not all social workers would necessarily go along with this. Some, for example, might feel that they have a role in social reform, a responsibility to try and change the environment rather than to adjust the client to it.
26 The Youth Leader falls in the middle for this role has both diffuse and specific elements: it can combine both counselling and the organization of clear-cut recreational activities. But whether diffuseness or specificity predominate depends on the setting: a peripatetic Youth Leader engaged in casework or group work with gangs will be far closer to social work than one responsible for a centre which offers membership only to children pursuing a specific hobby.

References

Albemarle Report (1960), *see* National Youth Employment Council.
—— (1965), *see* National Youth Employment Council.
Alexander, W. (1969), *Towards a New Education Act*, Councils and Education Press.
A.T.C.D.E. (1970), *Higher Education and Preparation for Teaching*.
A.U.T. (1970), *Universities in the 1970s*.
Bantock, G. H. (1967), 'The school and mental health', in *Education, Culture and the Emotions*, Faber & Faber.
Biestek, F. P. (1961), *The Casework Relationship*, Allen & Unwin.
Blyth, W. A. L. (1967), *English Primary Education*, Routledge & Kegan Paul.
Board of Education (1925), *Report of the Departmental Committee on the Training of Teachers for Public Elementary Schools*, H.M.S.O.
Bullock, A. (1970), reported in the *Guardian*, 30 January 1970.
Bulman, I., Craft, M., Milson, F. (1970), eds., *Youth Service and Interprofessional Studies*, Pergamon.
Carter, C. (1970), reported in the *Observer*, 11 January 1970.
Central Advisory Council for Education (1963), *Half our Future* (Newsom Report), H.M.S.O.
—— (1967), *Children and their Primary Schools* (Plowden Report), H.M.S.O.
Central Statistical Office (1969), *Annual Abstract of Statistics: 1969*, H.M.S.O.

Committee of Vice-Chancellors (1970), *University Development in the 1970s.*

Committee on Higher Education (1963), *Higher Education* (Robbins Report), H.M.S.O.

Committee on Local Authority and Allied Personal Social Services (1968), *Report* (Seebohm Report), Cmnd 3703.

Craft, M. (1967), 'Education and social work', in Pedley, F. H., ed., *Education and Social Work*, Pergamon.

Craft, M. (1969), 'The identity of the teacher: a commentary', in Taylor, W. (1969a), *op. cit.*

Craft, M. (1970a), ed., *Family, Class and Education*, Longman.

Craft, M. (1970b), 'Developments in interprofessional training', in *Higher Education Journal*, Vol. 17, No. 3.

Cross Report (1888), *see* Royal Commission on the Elementary Education Acts.

D.E.S. (1955), *Report of the Committee on Maladjusted Children*, H.M.S.O.

—— (1965), *Administrative Memorandum 7/65*, H.M.S.O.

—— (1966), *Report of the Study Group on Government of Colleges of Education* (Weaver Report), H.M.S.O.

—— (1968), *Reports on Education: No. 49*, H.M.S.O.

—— (1969a), *Statistics of Education: 1967*, H.M.S.O.

—— (1969b), *Statistics of Education: 1968*, H.M.S.O.

—— (1969c), *Reports on Education: No. 53*, H.M.S.O.

—— (1969d), *Youth and Community Work in the 1970s*, H.M.S.O.

—— (1970), *Education and Science in 1969*, H.M.S.O.

Departmental Committee on the Probation Service (1962) (*Second Report*))(Morison Report), Cmnd 1800.

Fabian Society (1970), *Planning for Education in 1980.*

Foren, R., and Bailey, R. (1968), *Authority in Social Casework*, Pergamon.

Gibbs, N. (1959), 'Reflections on the conferences at Keele and Leicester', in Halmos, P. (1959), *op. cit.*

Goldthorpe, J. H., *et al.* (1969), *The Affluent Worker in the Class Structure*, Cambridge University Press.

Gulbenkian Foundation (1968), *Community Work and Social Change*, Longman.

Halmos, P. (1959), *Sociological Review Monograph No. 2*, University of Keele.

Hollis, F. (1940), *Social Casework in Practice*, New York: Family Service Association of America.

Kelsall, R. K. (1970), *Population*, Longman.

Layard, R., King, J., Moser, C. (1969), *The Impact of Robbins*, Penguin Books.

Leonard, P. (1965), 'Social control, class values and social work practice', in *Social Work*, Vol. 22.

—— (1966), 'Social workers and bureaucracy', in *New Society* (2 June).

Maclure, S. (1968), *Learning Beyond Our Means?*, Councils and Education Press.

McNair Report (1944), *see* Ministry of Education.
Marsh, D. C. (1965), *The Changing Social Structure of England and Wales, 1871–1961*, Routledge & Kegan Paul.
Meyer, H. J., Litwak, E., Warren, D. (1968), 'Occupational and class differences in social values: a comparison of teachers and social workers', in *Sociology of Education*, Vol. 41, No. 3.
Ministry of Education (1944), *Teachers and Youth Leaders* (McNair Report), H.M.S.O.
Morison Report (1962), *see* Departmental Committee on the Probation Service.
Musgrove, F., and Taylor, P. H. (1969), *Society and the Teacher's Role*, Routledge & Kegan Paul.
National Youth Employment Council (1960), *The Youth Service in England and Wales* (Albemarle Report), H.M.S.O.
—— (1965), *The Future Development of the Youth Employment Council* (Albemarle Report), H.M.S.O.
Newsom Report (1963), *see* Central Advisory Council for Education.
Nokes, P. (1967), *The Professional Task in Welfare Practice*, Routledge & Kegan Paul.
Nursten, J. (1965), 'Social work, social class and speech systems', in *Social Work*, Vo. 22.
N.U.T. (1969), *The Future of Teacher Education.*
N.U.T. (1970), *Teacher Education: the Way Ahead.*
Parsons, T. (1951), *The Social System*, Routledge & Kegan Paul.
Pedley, R. (1969), *The Comprehensive University*, University of Exeter.
Plant, R. (1970), *Social and Moral Theory in Casework*, Routledge & Kegan Paul.
Plowden Report (1967), *see* Central Advisory Council for Education.
Rée, H. (1970), 'The making of a teacher' in the *Guardian*, 6 January 1970.
Robbins Report (1963), *see* Committee on Higher Education.
Robinson, E. (1968), *The New Polytechnics*, Penguin Books.
Royal Commission on the Elementary Education Acts (1888), *Report* (Cross Report), C. 5485.
Scottish Education Department (1968), *Community of Interests*, H.M.S.O.
Seebohm Report (1968), *see* Committee on Local Authority and Allied Personal Social Services.
Select Committee on Education and Science (1969, 1970), *Teacher Training: Minutes of Evidence*, H.M.S.O.
Taylor, R. K. (1958), 'The social control function in casework', in *Social Casework.*
Taylor, W. (1969a), *Towards a Policy for the Education of Teachers*, Butterworths.
—— (1969b), *Society and the Education of Teachers*, Faber & Faber.
Tibble, J. W. (1959), 'Problems in the training of teachers and social workers', in *Sociological Review Monograph No. 2*, University of Keele.

—— (1967), 'Interprofessional training', in Craft, M., *et al.* (1967), eds., *Linking Home and School*, Longman.

Timms, N. (1968), *The Language of Social Casework*, Routledge & Kegan Paul.

Toomey, D. M. (1969), 'Home-centred working class parents' attitudes towards their sons' education and careers', in *Sociology*, Vol. 3, No. 3.

Vaizey, J., and Sheehan, J. (1968), *Resources for Education*, Allen & Unwin.

Weaver Report (1966), *see* D.E.S. (1966).

Wilson, B. R. (1962), 'The teacher's role—a sociological analysis', in *British Journal of Sociology*, Vol. 13, No. 1.

Two	**The Colleges:**
	Prospects and
S. Hewett	**Possibilities**

The decision to meet the crisis in the supply of teachers between 1960 and 1970 by expansion of existing forms of training rather than temporary 'emergency' schemes produced the most remarkable growth record in the history of English full-time higher education. In 1957 the number of students in training stood at 27,000 and rose to 116,000 in 1970–71. The ingenious variety of methods by which this growth was achieved is indicative of the determination of central and local government and the colleges themselves to ensure that the statutory system of education should survive with standards unimpaired. New colleges were opened; departments of education were opened in certain technical colleges; existing colleges 'crowded-up', established outposts and annexes, and also introduced organizational changes which enabled teaching facilities to be used more intensively. The colleges may not have achieved the King of Brobdingnag's idea of making 'two blades of grass grow where only one grew before' but Box and Cox certainly enabled seven students to be taught where there was only room for six.

With the immediate crisis in teacher supply apparently over and with the present phase of expansion reaching completion, 1970 is an appropriate moment to review the effects on the colleges of the rapid expansion of the last ten years and to consider prospects and possibilities for the colleges in the future.

The most outstanding feature is that in spite of all the difficulties consequent on expansion, reorganization and the inevitable academic negotiations, the colleges have raised the level of their work and diversified their academic and professional courses. Almost as soon as the first three-year trained students left in 1963, B.Ed. courses for their successors were being devised. The colleges have now, in spite of occasional difficulties, firmly established their B.Ed. courses and have clearly demonstrated that they can undertake work at first degree level of honours standard. Similarly they have amply demonstrated their capacity to teach courses leading to the award of the Post-Graduate Certificate of Education. They are, in fact, carrying the major part of the expanded provision of these courses made necessary

D

by the decision to make professional training compulsory for graduates who wish to teach in maintained schools.

Together with this raising of academic and professional standards has gone a rapid development in the degree of academic self-government which the colleges can exercise. College Instruments and Articles of Government have been revised to make college academic boards mandatory and they have been given wide ranging powers over the ordering of their internal academic affairs. The development of higher level courses and the growth of academic responsibility have associated the colleges more closely with the universities than ever before. As well as the formal links of the Area Training Organization there is also a substantial degree of overlap in the work of colleges and universities and shared assumptions on the nature of academic responsibility.

Another distinctive feature which has emerged is that while all colleges have expanded to meet the crisis in the supply of teachers, some have expanded far more than others. We now have 164 institutions which range in size from 200 to 1800 students and which range in situation from rural, near isolation, to densely urban environments. The character of the institutions varies from day colleges with an extremely high proportion of mature students to large, residential colleges with few older students. In some colleges the proportion of B.Ed. students reaches 20 per cent of the total, in others the B.Ed. students are less than 5 per cent of the total and a few colleges feel that they cannot offer B.Ed. courses at all at the moment. The degree and range of all these differences are such that the colleges vary far more in their resources and character than they once did and it is increasingly difficult to use the term 'the colleges' as a meaningful abstraction.

Not surprisingly, the colleges have, over the last ten years, retained the basic tripartitite structure of the course of training which consists of the concurrent study of the theory and practice of education, a main subject or subjects, and curriculum or professional studies. Periods of rapid, even hectic, expansion are not the most suitable times for major revision of course structures and patterns of training. Considerable variation of content and treatment exists within this basic framework and colleges differ considerably in the allocation of time between the three basic areas, but the basic structure itself exists though some of the assumptions which led to its establishment are being increasingly questioned.

The colleges have also become acutely aware of the number of partners in the teacher education 'consortium' all of whom have views on how the colleges should conduct their work. The colleges have to meet the academic demands of universities within the administrative and financial framework set by central and local government. This separation of academic and professional ends from administrative and financial means is a constant dilemma for the colleges. In addition to these three 'masters' the colleges are expected to be responsive to the views of teachers and students on the nature and purposes of teacher education. These multiple and frequently conflicting demands ensure that some degree of dissatisfaction with the work of the colleges must exist somewhere. It is ironic that at a time when the quality of work in the colleges is higher than it has ever been the demands for an 'enquiry' have been strongest. The variety of those demands and the conflicting criticisms which give rise to them are perhaps a reflection of the lack of consensus on the aims of education and hence the kinds of teachers required to help achieve them. They certainly illustrate that no sector of higher education is as exposed to multiple demands as the colleges and may well be in the last analysis as much a criticism of the system under which colleges have to work as a criticism of the work itself.

As the colleges reach this point in their history the national systems of higher education would appear to be facing a decade of major expansion. If the policy of making higher education available to all qualified candidates who wish to avail themselves of it is to be maintained over the next decade, it would appear that provision must be made for at least 325,000 places in higher education by 1971. The place of teacher education within this total expansion is of crucial importance and the future development of the colleges must be considered in relation to the general content of higher education and not in isolation from it.

The prime duty of the colleges is to safeguard the quality of entrants to the teaching profession. A prerequisite for this is to ensure that the teaching profession recruits from the higher levels of intellectual ability and academic attainment. Failure to do this would mean that national aspirations in the field of education would have little hope of fulfilment.

In order to ensure that potential teachers of adequate calibre are recruited, minimum entrance qualifications to colleges of education are set, the minimum qualification at the moment being passes in five subjects in the General Certificate of Education at Ordinary level. In 1960–61, 16·4 per cent of the relevant age-group had an academic attainment of five Ordinary level passes or better and only 6·9 per cent had two or more Advanced level passes. The colleges at that time were therefore recruiting from the ablest 16 per cent of the age-group and, since a substantial number of their students had Advanced level qualifications as well, were able to be selective even within that band. The present prediction of the Department of Education and Science is that by 1975, 16·7 per cent of school leaves will be obtaining two or more 'A' levels and by 1980 the percentage will rise to 20·2.

If the teaching profession is to recruit in 1975 entrants from the same band of ability as they did in 1960, i.e. the top 16 per cent, the colleges should set as minimum entrance requirements two Advanced level passes. Since teaching is becoming an increasingly complex and demanding profession one would hope that the colleges would be able to become increasingly selective rather than less selective in their recruitment. When, by 1980, 20 per cent of the relevant age-group is likely to have two or more Advanced level passes it will be absolutely essential for the colleges to set entrance qualifications which will ensure that all their recruits, apart from exceptional cases, come from the 20 per cent so qualified. The education system of an advanced and developed nation could not be sustained by a teaching profession whose members were drawn from below the top 20 per cent of intellectual ability. To ensure the quality of entrants to the teaching profession the colleges should, as soon as possible, and certainly not later than 1975–6 set the same minimum entry qualifications as those demanded by universities and by the degree courses of the C.N.A.A. A single minimum entry qualification to all courses of higher education would simplify the admission procedures of the higher education jungle and would help to remove the unfortunate distinctions which now exist.

The prospect of doubling the provision of higher education over the next ten years within the expenditure likely to be available is a challenging one which must involve radical rethinking of the nature and purposes of higher education and the fullest utilization of all existing resources. In the reshaping of the higher education system to accommodate one-fifth of the relevant age-groups the existing colleges of education should play a vital part.

There is a growing feeling that many existing honours courses fail to meet the real needs of a substantial number of existing students. Relatively few look upon their undergraduate work as preparation for further academic study at post-graduate level and increasing numbers require more broadly based studies which would give them the intellectual flexibility to face with confidence and maturity an increasingly complex world of work and leisure. The vast expansion of higher education now being contemplated would, almost certainly, increase the number of students whose needs were not adequately catered for by existing courses. 'More' means 'different' rather than 'worse'. The colleges of education could make a valuable contribution to the diversification of undergraduate courses which should be a pronounced feature of the expanded provision of higher education.

The colleges have certain strengths which could be developed to complement and supplement, rather than compete with, existing provision and could make a distinctive contribution to the range of undergraduate courses rather than offering replicas of traditional honours courses. The colleges have considerable experience of inter-disciplinary and grouped courses and have traditionally placed great emphasis on the quality of their teaching, though not to the exclusion of further study and research. The rapid development of their education departments and the increasing tendency to appoint specialist staff to them means that they are now well placed to develop broadly based courses in the social and behavioural sciences with a strong practical bias though not necessarily confined to the schools. Applications to university departments of sociology, psychology and applied social studies and the development of 'A' level courses in the first two subjects would seem to indicate that in the area of social and behavioural sciences demand for places is likely to exceed supply.

In addition the colleges have a strong tradition in the creative and performing arts, areas which universities and the technical colleges (from which the new polytechnics are emerging) have, for historical reasons, neglected. The existing courses in art, craft, music, drama, physical education, dance and movement could be further developed to provide areas of study, experience and creativity which have traditionally been excluded to a large extent from higher education and left for specialist institutions to provide.

The work which the colleges have developed in the more traditional fields of the humanities and sciences has acquired its own distinctive characteristics which are different though not inferior to courses in those fields in other institutions. The total range of courses which the colleges now offer would permit the development of broadly based courses in the sciences, the humanities, the creative arts and social/behavioural studies which would permit a considerable element of inter-disciplinary work. Such courses terminating in a degree award could provide a satisfactory higher education and could also be eminently suitable for the large number of students who would see their degrees as preparation for professional postgraduate courses of various kinds including teaching.

On educational grounds, there seems a strong case for closely involving the colleges in the expansion of higher education and giving them a proportionate share of the 325,000 target figure. But there are also economic arguments which should not be ignored. The colleges as a whole are cost-effective compared with other areas of higher education.

> Between 1961–2 and 1966–7 university costs per student at current prices rose from £601 to £941—by 57 per cent. The rise in colleges of education was much less—well below 20 per cent, and on top of this there were sharp economies in the provision of accommodation. It is interesting to compare these increases in cost per student with those of 32 per cent in primary schools and 55 per cent in secondary.
>
> Stuart Maclure, *Learning Beyond Our Means?*

While the colleges regard their prize for cost-effectiveness as a dubious honour it would appear that their utilization would make a significant contribution to holding down the costs of the expansion of higher education over the next decade.

Participation in the expansion of higher education and the development of courses of the kind outlined in no way means that the colleges would abandon their present function of preparing teachers for work in primary and secondary schools. Their evolution into multi-purpose institutions would however involve an adjustment of their curricula to cater for a wider variety of students than they do at present. A large number of students would be committed to teaching on entry, others might elect to train for teaching at some point during their course, others might so choose at the end of their undergraduate course, others might choose to leave merely with a degree without any form of professional training. A structure of courses far more flexible than that which exists at the moment would be needed to cater for the varying and changing needs of the student population we are likely to encounter. There is evidence that young men and women are increasingly reluctant to commit themselves to teaching on entry to college and one suspects that of those who have apparently committed themselves a number are 'at college' rather than fully committed to a life-time career in teaching. It may well be that they are seeking the only form of higher education open to them rather than professional training. A system which allowed students to delay commitment would be of real value to many and would 'legitimize' the presence of yet others.

Adapting existing college curricula to cater for the varieties of categories of students outlined would not be a major task, since all the elements from which they would be constructed are already in existence. The problem is one of reorganizing the relation of the parts to the whole and building in a variety of choices. It is likely that in the early stages of reorganization at least the certificate course would continue to exist both as a terminal qualification for those unsuited to degree work and also as Part I of the B.Ed. course. Alongside this basic three-year course would exist courses leading to the award of degrees in the faculties of art, sciences and social sciences with ample opportunity for two-way transfer between degree and certificate courses. A variety of postgraduate professional courses could exist to prepare graduates for work in a variety of professional fields (see Table 3, p. 25 above).

The precise way in which individual colleges steered their courses between the Scylla of flexibility and the Charybdis of rigidity could vary considerably without violating the basic principles. Some colleges might arrange to have the first two years of all courses in common and thus delay 'branching' until the end of the second year. Others might prefer to have elements common to both routes and thus facilitate exchange and transfer. Others might adopt the principle that any total course is an approved combination of shorter courses and provide a wide range of courses in years one, two and three from which students would choose combinations appropriate to their developing interests and/or vocational goals. This method would give students the opportunity of exercising a measure of control over the total course they build for themselves out of the range of shorter courses available, though some limitation would need to be imposed by a college to ensure that a given qualification was preceded by adequate study in appropriate fields.

The development of course units which, appropriately combined, would produce a total course would be a rewarding one for the colleges to consider. In spite of the options which exist within courses, higher education in England is to a large extent a Procrustean bed to which the student must be fitted by process of mutilation if need be. We tend to look for 'horses for courses' rather than devise 'courses for horses'. There is a danger that overmuch flexibility would produce a lack of coherence in a student's studies but this could be controlled by the size of the units offered and the limitations placed upon his choice. Larger units make for greater coherence and 'vertical restrictions' which prescribe the sequence in which certain units are taken, together with 'horizontal restrictions' which prescribe which units may or may not be taken simultaneously could maintain the coherence of students' courses without destroying flexibility entirely.

The unit system would have distinct advantages for professional training since it would enable students preparing for different kinds of teaching to differentiate their courses in an appropriate way. Students preparing for work with younger children would be able, if they so wished, to take the bulk of their work from the area of the social and behavioural sciences together with substantial units of school-based experience and reduce the number of units taken from the humanities and the sciences. At present they are committed to a main subject for the same number of hours per week as a potential subject specialist in a secondary school. Potential secondary or middle-school teachers would adjust in appropriate ways the balance of their respective courses.

Such a system might also end the sharp distinction which at present exists between end-on and concurrent training. At the moment end-on courses seem to involve three years of irrelevance followed by an intensive year of alleged relevance. Concurrent courses are supposed to be continually relevant, though main subjects in some institutes proclaim their irrelevance to professional preparation. Within a unit system the student could, within limitations, control the amount and kind of professional relevance within his course. Similarly an undergraduate student uncommitted to teaching but with an eye on the possibility

might well select courses from the field of the social and behavioural sciences which would make a satisfactory course of
study in itself and also be an admirable theoretical and practical
base for professional postgraduate training. Courses for the Post-
Graduate Certificate of Education would in all probability need
to be differentiated more than they are at present to take account of
the students' undergraduate experience which would be of considerable advantage to both tutors and students.

Colleges would need to be related to other institutions for the
validation of their work and the award of qualifications since it is
unlikely in the foreseeable future that they would be chartered
to award their own degrees and certificates. The choice lies
between university awards, as with the B.Ed. at present, and
qualifications awarded by the C.N.A.A. The case for strengthening, extending and developing the college-university link seems
the stronger.

Since the setting up of the Institutes of Education in the wake
of the McNair Report the colleges' links with their universities
have become steadily stronger and closer. The initial discussions in
Subject Advisory Committees quickly showed that universities
were sympathetic to the colleges' desire to devise their own
syllabuses to meet the particular needs of their students and the
particular strength of their staffs. This freedom was re-affirmed
when schemes of work and syllabuses were revised for the introduction of the three-year course in 1960. Regulations were established for each A.T.O. within which the colleges had considerable
freedom to develop individualized content and approach. This
variety within a common basis pattern is one of the most distinctive features of the work of the colleges. The vast majority of
universities were no less generous when B.Ed. courses came to
be devised after 1964. Universities have, with rare exceptions,
accepted for undergraduate study courses which often they themselves do not teach such as art, craft, physical education, dance,
movement and home economics. The courses devised are as
demanding in their own way as more traditional undergraduate
courses and such subjects are now being taken seriously in university circles. The stigma of the second-class subject in which it
was not possible to graduate is being removed.

In addition, many universities have been generous in amend-
ing matriculation regulations and permitting exceptional entry.
Furthermore the setting up of B.Ed. courses for serving teachers

is now proceeding in many universities and both full-time and part-time courses (and combinations of both) are being devised. The discussion and negotiation of all these facilities has resulted in a closer working relationship between colleges and universities and a deeper mutual understanding than has ever existed before. It would seem folly to reverse the accelerating developments of the last twenty-five years and send colleges elsewhere for their academic sponsorship. It would seem wiser to extend the links which now relate universities and colleges and thus permit the colleges to teach for degrees in faculties other then education. The basic structure of such a system already exists and could be built upon without raising radically new issues of principle.

Since the relationship between a central institution and its constituent colleges is dependent to a large degree on the individual contacts which the structure permits there is a strong case for increasing the number of universities which are associated with colleges. A large number of universities have been established since the A.T.O. structure was devised and the existing pattern has neither logic nor economy to commend it. Not infrequently colleges with universities on their doorstep look to universities some distance away for their academic and professional guidance. The involvement of many more universities would make for smaller, more cohesive units thus simplifying administrative procedures and resulting in closer working relationships.

The concept of a federated group of colleges associated with a parent university could be a profitable one from the point of view of rationalization of resources. Within any particular group the situation, character and resources of the various colleges might vary considerably. It could be useful to consider them collectively to rationalize the most effective contribution each might make to the overall provision of higher education facilities within the area which contains the group. The largest colleges could perhaps develop still further and offer the full range of possibilities and approach in size and scale of operation the old style university colleges. Others might find it more suitable to restrict the range of their activities and concentrate on preparation for teaching and in-service provision. Others might find that local circumstances and existing strength suggested that they should develop their strength still further and offer a restricted range of work but to a high level. Distance from the parent university need not rule out extensive development. Indeed, certain colleges at some distance from the university might well be built into major collegiate institutions in order to bring to an area the social and cultural benefits which contact with universities provide but which many areas are at present denied. Such colleges might well become bases for university extra-mural departments and study centres for the Open University.

Whatever forms rationalization within a given area might or might not take, the university and its colleges have a total set of resources which should be developed in such a way that each institution can make its distinctive contribution to the whole in the way that is culturally, educationally and economically most desirable. It should be possible within such a structure to transfer students between institutions should their original choice of course prove unsuitable, and thus wastage could be kept to a minimum. Viewed in this way additional undergraduate places in the colleges as a result of the expansion could be regarded in a sense as university places decentralized to constituent institutions.

The advantages of federation would not be confined to the colleges. There is evidence that universities, through their closer contact with the colleges, as a result of co-operation over the B.Ed. have not only become aware of problems which they had hitherto regarded as outside their concern but also interested in finding solutions to them. University staffs outside education departments are now more deeply concerned with what goes on in the schools and the kind of people who work in them than they have been in the past. That they should regard education as a continuum rather than something which starts at eighteen is all to the good and one would hope that this interest would have the opportunity to develop further. Moreover, the decentralization of some part of their expansion might well suit some universities which could find extension of central campuses in urban environments not only prohibitively expensive but also productive of urban over-crowding with all its associated tensions. In addition the colleges might well provide the kind of broadly based courses which some universities with their largely departmental arrangements could find difficult to offer.

The system outlined is not dependent upon the colleges being financed through the University Grants Committee though some readjustment of the methods by which the colleges are financed is necessary to avoid the perennial difficulties caused by separation of academic ends and financial means. At present financial and administrative control of L.E.A. colleges is exercised at two levels, national and local. The setting up of the Committee on Pooled Expenditure to standardize costs in colleges of education is evidence that the existing system whereby individual local authorities are responsible for the financial administration of L.E.A. colleges with money drawn from a national pool has proved grossly inefficient and has led to unacceptable variation in standards of provision. The existence of the Committee on Pooled Expenditure seems to argue the need for centralized control of finance and more equitable arrangements for the colleges. It is difficult therefore to see why local supervision of expenditure is also necessary. It would not be difficult to modify the decentralized arrangements so that the existing committee became a Colleges' Grants Committee on which college representatives were in a majority. From such a committee recurrent and capital monies could be channelled directly to the colleges and the financial and academic responsibilities would at long last be united. The principle of 'direct grant' is not a new one in the colleges since the voluntary colleges have long been financed in this way. The setting up of a Colleges' Grants Committee would do more than almost anything else to enable the colleges to develop as major institutions of higher education. Since the colleges would have certain specific roles to fulfil they would naturally have to accept that a high proportion of their grant would be earmarked for these specific purposes.

The participation of the colleges of education in the expansion of higher education and the consequent liberalization and diversification of their function would break down the isolation in which they have been kept since their institution. This in its turn would remove the feeling that exists within the teaching profession that, for the most part, its members were forced into an early commitment and given a qualification which had no validity outside teaching. The profession would draw its recruits from people who had made their decision to join it at a more mature age with a fuller awareness of other possibilities.

The raising of entry qualifications to the minimum demanded by the universities would bring within striking distance the long-sought goal of an all-graduate profession and the greater flexibility of course structure would enable more differentiated and hence more specific professional preparation to be undertaken.

For the last twenty-five years supply considerations have dominated all discussions on the education of teachers and the nature of their professional training has been a secondary consideration. The task of the colleges is not to ensure supply but to provide the best possible preparation for those who wish to avail themselves of it. The responsibility for ensuring supply rests with those who are responsible for the operation of the statutory system of education. Hitherto supply has been assured by the 'captive audience' of the college population and the special 'protectionist' measures which are associated with mono-vocational institutions. If in the future teaching is to achieve the full status of a profession it must no longer depend on the 'captive audience' for its recruits but must compete in the open market for its members.

The task facing the system of higher education at the moment is to make the most suitable provision it can for the rapidly increasing number of young men and women who wish to continue their education after the age of eighteen and the colleges have a vital role to play in this vast undertaking. One of their main tasks will be to provide the best professional preparation they can for those who wish to make a career in teaching. It is the task of the teachers and their employers to create a profession which is sufficiently attractive to ensure that enough young people will want to do so.

The colleges have had a long history. Most of the voluntary colleges and many of the maintained colleges have longer histories than many existing universities. In the later stages of their existence they have grown considerably in number and in size but they cannot be said to have developed. They retain the same limited function now that they had at their inception though their methods of performing it have changed radically. They have now reached the point where they must use their achievements and tradition as a base for development beyond their original function or gradually fade from the scene. The solution of the crisis in supply achieved over the last ten years and the expansion of higher education over the next ten years provide the first and perhaps the last opportunity for them to do this. The colleges are now of sufficient standing to be able to contemplate with confidence new areas of achievement and the increased number of students for whom provision will have to be made could give them the material with which to do so. If the colleges can share as full partners in the

expansion of higher education over the next decade the consequences will go far beyond the colleges themselves. The system of
higher education will have acquired a new flexibility and the
profession will have come in from the cold.

Three	**The Objectives and**
	Structure of the
Peter Renshaw	**College Curriculum**

The function of a college of education

In this chapter the argument will be limited to a discussion of the principles that underlie the structure of the concurrent certificate course in colleges of education. My main thesis is that the college of education, by virtue of its dual concern with academic and professional studies, has a distinctive role to perform. Each institution within tertiary education needs to be viewed as an entity with its own unique function and educational autonomy within a unitary national system. The main purpose of a university, for instance, is to cultivate a spirit of critical enquiry and to develop in students the desire to pursue knowledge for its intrinsic value. A university is concerned with the life of the intellect and with building up a community of scholars and students engaged in the task of seeking truth. Colleges of technology and polytechnics, on the other hand, are multi-vocational institutions, which encompass a great variety of professional education and training.

But the college of education, as constituted at present, has a unique character resulting from its dual function in the education and training of students for the sole profession of teaching. Although one of its objectives is to develop those qualities of mind associated with a university education, both staff and students are bound by a distinctive professional commitment. In a college of education those academic studies designed for the education of students as persons may be pursued for their intrinsic value, but because of the nature of the institution these studies may be structured to have professional significance. Instead of the dichotomy that tends to exist between academic and professional studies, there should be a very close relationship between the education and training of the student. But this raises several pertinent questions. What do we understand by academic and professional study in a college of education? Furthermore, in what ways can a college curriculum be structured to emphasize the interrelationships between academic and professional studies, thus helping to forge the link between theory and practice?

Academic study in a college of education

In colleges academic study has been traditionally associated with the main subject, its central concern being the 'personal development' of the student.[1] When the revised course for the Teacher's Certificate was introduced in 1949 the main subject was conceived 'primarily for its value in the personal development of the student, and not necessarily having any direct connection with his teaching work'.[2] Its professional relevance was recognized for secondary specialist teachers in 1963,[3] but it has continued to have very little professional significance for the primary student-teacher.

This conception of the main subject has led to some unfortunate results. In many cases courses have been modelled on the traditional pattern of the university honours school, thus investing the main subject with a status that has tended to separate academic and professional studies. But why must the idea of academic study be limited to the main subject? Furthermore, in a teacher education curriculum might it not be more appropriate to view academic study as an integral part of professional study? In which case, perhaps the idea of 'personal development' might embrace both types of study and not be limited to the main subject. Let us examine these questions in greater detail.

First, what do we understand by the concept 'person'? This is, of course, an enormous philosophical problem, but I would suggest that central to the idea of a person is man's capacity to reflect on himself as a person and to grasp the relationship between himself and the world. In other words, a person is a centre of consciousness whose awareness gradually develops into a deeper understanding of the different modes of thought and feeling that constitute the basis of our civilization. The notion 'personal development' partly implies that man's simplistic view of the world is refined and widened as he builds up elaborate conceptual structures and learns to make more sophisticated discriminations in his experience. As his understanding is transformed he develops certain qualities of mind, values and beliefs as to what is worth-while, and he learns to evaluate his actions according to rational principles. A stage is reached when he can formulate intentions, make responsible choices and use reason in acting and judging. This quest for reasons and justifications gradually 'frees' a person from external authority, and the central concern becomes the search for truth and the development of a personal autonomy based on reason.

But, although rational autonomy is central to a student's personal development, other qualities are also important if he is to gain the balanced personality and the breadth of maturity so necessary for teaching. For instance, emotional stability, self-control, personal insight, the ability to establish interpersonal relationships, and sensitivity towards other people's interests and feelings—all form part of the development of a person, but they will hardly be acquired through the study of one main subject, or even through a range of subjects. In order to develop such qualities, not only a variety of teaching experiences with children is needed, but also the college itself should create an 'open' atmosphere and present a wide range of liberalizing experiences aimed at maturing the students as people, broadening their outlook and giving them a realistic understanding of the world outside teaching.

The central point in this argument is that the concept 'personal development' embraces a range of qualities that cannot be realized through the academic study of a main subject alone. Some, in fact, could not be developed through the curriculum at all, as they are more likely to be the result of social and emotional experiences outside college or within the student-staff community.

Undoubtedly, the objective systematic study of an area of knowledge pursued in depth for intrinsic reasons can contribute to the personal development of the student. Such study should enable a person to reflect critically on the logic and nature of his discipline, to master the appropriate validation procedures and to view its distinctive characteristics in relation to other forms of understanding. This submission of the mind to the rigorous canons of a form of thought not only brings a student to the point of asking fundamental questions concerning the value, standards, methods, assumptions and scope of the activity, but it also enables him to build up a personal commitment to the discipline so that it becomes significant to him. This care and respect for a form of thought can contribute to both the mastery of the subject and to the development of personal knowledge within that discipline. Academic study, then, can give students the opportunity to develop such qualities of mind as rationality, autonomy, judgment, imagination, critical and logical thought, but these qualities can be understood only in relation to a specific area of knowledge.[4]

E

Aesthetic judgment, for instance, is logically distinct from moral or mathematical judgment. Imagination in history is different in kind from imagination in literature or biology. Since no discipline can develop these qualities *in general*, the experiences gained from studying one main subject can contribute only to a small part of a student's personal development. In other words, if a student is 'to realize himself as a person' he needs to submit himself to a far wider range of experiences than can be provided by the academic study of one main subject. In fact, the idea of 'academic study' need not be confined to one subject; whilst the notion 'personal development' embraces a variety of experiences which include both academic and professional study, thereby cutting across all aspects of the college curriculum, as well as extending outside it.

This view can be substantiated if we examine what is entailed in 'learning how to teach'. Essentially, teaching is an ability which involves developing a critical skill in order to give an intelligent performance. This skill is guided by a body of theoretical knowledge, rules and principles which needs to be acquired through academic study. But building up technical competence through training and critical practice is also a disciplined activity, in which a student learns how to make independent judgments, to formulate intentions and to make rational choices. In other words, rational autonomy, which is a central feature of 'personal development', can be achieved not only through reading a main subject, but also through the academic study of education and in the practical activity of teaching. Further, moreover, good teaching requires the ability to gain a relationship with children based on respect for each child as a person and on impartiality. Any constraints imposed on children must be capable of rational justification. In fact, the very concept 'teaching' implies respecting a pupil's judgment, welcoming critical discussion and being prepared to offer rational explanations. These qualities, attitudes and values associated with good teaching must be considered essential to the personal development of the student, but they are acquired through the study of educational theory partnered by school experience. This example of 'learning how to teach' should help to demonstrate the absurdity of limiting the idea of 'personal development' to the study of a main subject.

The concept 'personal development', then, embraces both academic and professional study, and includes those experiences gained from extra-curricular activities and the life of the institution in general. The notion of 'academic study' is limited in its scope, but not so narrow as to be identified solely with the main subject. For instance, it also has a significant role in the theoretical study of education and in certain elements of the curriculum courses. Furthermore, as the college of education has a professional objective, all academic study ought to be conceived within a professional frame of reference; it ought not to be pursued for intrinsic reasons alone.[5]

Professional study in a college of education

Essentially, the idea of 'professional study' implies a partnership between a body of theoretical knowledge and the practical skills which are needed for achieving competence in a particular profession. The development of these critical skills, acquired through training, must be informed by theoretical knowledge gained through academic study, otherwise a student is unlikely to build up the authority, autonomy and breadth of understanding which are so fundamental to the making of responsible professional judgments. Professional study is not limited to the development of technical competence in a narrow, specific task, for the partnership between theoretical and practical knowledge is central to the idea of initiating students into a profession, rather than training them for a trade or occupation. Therefore a balance between theory and practice needs to be maintained in professional study but, as much of the theoretical knowledge must be acquired through academic study, there also needs to be a close relationship between academic and professional studies.

In a college of education, with its dual function of educating and training students for a profession, certain conflicts and tensions are likely to arise in the process of achieving this balance. For instance, study for its intrinsic value as opposed to that with an instrumental end; theoretical as distinct from practical activity; differences in understanding between schools and colleges, as well as between subject and education departments. Individual lecturers and students will also be involved in a constant inner dialogue between academic and professional commitments. Nevertheless, a sharp dichotomy need not arise if a close link be established between academic and professional studies. This should be feasible if it is understood that academic study need not stand in isolation, but is in fact an integral part of professional study.

Let me illustrate this central point of the argument with reference to the structure of the main subject, educational theory and the curriculum courses in colleges.

(a) *Main subject*

If students are to engage in academic study without sacrificing the idea of professional relevance, I would suggest that the main course contain four interrelated elements—the nature of the discipline; the place of the subject in education; the psychological aspects of learning the subject; and the subject matter for schools and teaching methods. Perhaps it ought to be pointed out that the criterion of 'professional relevance' in this context must not be interpreted solely in relation to the immediate practical needs of the classroom, for it can have a much wider connotation. Viewing the term in its broader sense, I would maintain that the interaction between academic and professional studies ought to be central to the main course, with the intention that disciplined theoretical study will impinge on educational practice. The sort of programme envisaged would necessitate joint planning and some team-teaching, thereby establishing strong lines of communication between subject and education departments, and between schools and colleges. Each component will be examined now in greater detail.

The academic study of the nature of the discipline would form the central core of the main course, thus providing the very necessary conceptual foundations prior to the examination of the more directly professional aspects of teaching the subject. What does such study entail? If a student is to learn to formulate concepts and to communicate in a discipline, knowledge of the basic facts, definitions, terms and symbols within the particular form of thought is essential.[6] In history, for example, knowledge of specific dates, events, persons, places and sources of information is necessary for the beginning of historical thinking. However, knowledge must not remain at this inert level, for a thorough grasp of the discipline can be achieved only by building up an understanding of the central concepts and fundamental ideas of the particular mode of thought.[7] Such concepts as causality, time, development and revolution in history, or form, rhythm, style and balance in aesthetics enable us to structure our experience in an economical and connected way.[8] This emphasis on economy of experience is important because if certain basic concepts and principles represent the main characteristics of a discipline, a sound knowledge of these ideas is more valuable than the learning of a large number of specific items of information. In other words, the understanding need not be gained from an encyclopaedic body of content, for the academic study may be concentrated on a few paradigm cases selected to exemplify the main features of the discipline. From these particular examples generalization may be drawn to show the range of understanding within the area of knowledge. This approach to a subject would also try to demonstrate that each mode of thought contains its own distinctive conceptual structure which binds it into a whole and defines its boundaries of enquiry. Furthermore, considerable emphasis would be placed on learning how to use the appropriate technical procedures for evaluating the truth of facts, principles and statements within the discipline.[9] In history, for instance, students would learn how historians collect evidence and how they use it to reconstruct and to interpret the unique events of the past. Through the handling of primary sources students would learn how to validate historical evidence, judge conflicting interpretations, detect bias and distinguish truth. This sort of academic study is not only of logical significance, but its professional relevance can also be demonstrated. For example, the subject matter studied can be selected to illustrate the main features and procedural skills of the discipline, as well as having relevance to the learning and teaching of history in schools. In addition, emphasis can be placed on making explicit the conceptual interconnections between areas of knowledge, thus building up a student's perspective, which is not only of intrinsic value but also essential for successful interdisciplinary work with children.

Although the critical examination of the nature of the discipline would form the centre of the main course, the other three components would enable the students especially to focus their academic study within a professional frame of reference. For instance, it is of central concern to explore the justification for including the area of knowledge in the school curriculum. What is the place of the subject in education? What are the principles underpinning the teaching of the subject in schools? This particular area of the main course needs to be related to a range of wider questions concerning educational justifications and curriculum objectives.

It could be argued that the logical and psychological aspects of learning and teaching are at the core of the work in a college, and thus the third component in the main course ought to be devoted to the psychological features that influence the learning of the particular subject. This must not be divorced from the education course, which needs to examine such relevant areas as human development, concept formation, the learning of different types of content, motivational factors in learning, educational technology, and evaluation procedures and testing. It is vital that these psychological principles be applied to the learning of the particular subject being studied.

In the fourth component of the main course, the theoretical aspects of learning and teaching the subject need to be related more directly to educational practice. For instance, students must have a grasp of the criteria that can be used for determining the selection of subject-matter, so that they have a realistic idea of the content appropriate for children at the different stages of their development. Finally, they need to build up a capital of practical knowledge including the teaching methods, classroom activities and audio-visual material that enable children to learn the facts, concepts, skills and procedures of the particular discipline.

(b) *Educational theory*

The aim of educational theory is to initiate students into those areas of knowledge which contribute to the formulation of principles that guide the solving of practical educational problems. Throughout this chapter it has been assumed that education can be studied academically, but the validity of this contention depends on the status and nature of educational theory. Until comparatively recently there has been a tendency to conceive of education as an autonomous unitary discipline.[10] But it is more logical to view it as a 'focus or meeting-place of disciplines',[11] or a 'practical theory',[12] which draws on a number of distinct areas of knowledge that contribute towards the making of practical judgments as to what ought to be done in educational practice. It is logically impossible for the contributory disciplines to be subsumed under a general unitary mode of understanding, because each area contains its own concepts, truth criteria and validation procedures. For instance, sociology and psychology use empirical evidence and statistical techniques to describe and explain certain states of affairs. Philosophy, on the other hand, is concerned with questions of meaning, patterns of argument and criteria of justification.

This differentiated approach has enabled the study of education, through its distinctive disciplines, to be truly academic. The formulation of rational principles must be achieved through the objective systematic study of the contributory disciplines. At some stage of the education course these must be pursued for intrinsic reasons; the emphasis must be on impartial academic enquiry, with its high concern for cognitive content, search for truth and the mastery of procedural skills. This sort of study must play an important part in the personal education of the student, but its professional significance must not be overlooked. The content must be selected not only to exemplify the main features of philosophy, psychology and so on, but also for its professional relevance.

The aim of philosophy of education during initial training, for example, is not to cultivate miniature philosophers, whose commitment to the discipline makes them blind to the realities of teaching in the classroom. What philosophy can do is to give students the conceptual apparatus with which to reflect critically and clearly on the nature of their job. By examining the use of language and the meaning of educational concepts, and through raising fundamental questions, seeking justifications, and challenging the basis of assumptions and value-judgments, a student-teacher can begin to build up an important dimension of his professional life.

The theoretical study of education, then, must be allied to a growing knowledge of children and schools. It must inform the teacher's professional judgments and actions, and provide him with a sufficient range of concepts and skills with which to evaluate the new ideas and research findings of educational innovation.

(c) *Curriculum courses*

Curriculum courses form the third area in which academic study can play a significant role in the professional education of the student. At present most students, from infant to junior/secondary, are exposed to a multiplicity of curriculum courses which act as an introduction to the basic content of a range of subjects, as well as giving insight into how to teach them. Many of these courses are of a factual nature, whilst others concentrate on teaching methodology; in many cases they are criticized as being superficial and intellectually undemanding, which is probably inevitable in the time available. This raises the fundamental question about the purpose and function of a curriculum course, and whether there is a need for subject lecturers, education tutors and teachers to work together more closely in order to draw out the logical and psychological aspects of teaching and learning a subject.

I would suggest that if academic and professional studies be conceived as an integral whole, the structure of a curriculum course might comprise three distinct and yet interrelated elements: conceptual, factual content and methodological. The conceptual aspect would emphasize fundamental ideas and principles, as it would focus on the nature of the particular activity and the justification for teaching it. The content would be selected to illustrate some of the salient features of the discipline, thus enabling students to move with confidence within a subject without having to digest an amorphous mass of inert information. The methodological element would concentrate on the procedural skills of the discipline, allied to the practical knowledge of how to teach. Thus a combination of the conceptual and factual elements, acquired through academic study would contribute to the personal education of the student, whilst all three components would be examined within a professional context thereby satisfying the criterion of relevance. Central to such a course is the recognition of the need to draw out the conceptual and practical relationships between educational theory, subjects and practice, because I would maintain that it is this knowledge of concepts, principles, structures, validation procedures and the ability to grasp interconnections that forms the essence of 'professionalism'.

But although this section has tried to demonstrate that academic study in a college of education may be conceived as an integral part of professional study, this is not to neglect the more practical dimension of an initial training programme. Professional study must also aim at building up a high level of technical expertise, but these skills required for teaching must be gained through training and practical experience. If teaching be characterized as a critical skill or 'intelligent capacity',[13] rather than a mere habit, the professional training of teachers must be concerned with both theoretical and practical knowledge, which entails the intelligent application of rules. The idea of an intelligent action suggests that a person is thinking in a purposive way; not only is his action related to an end but the appropriate means are being employed to achieve the end. An intelligently executed operation also involves judgment and understanding, thus enabling the person to give a critical performance. This means that when a person is being trained, he must learn how to apply the relevant rules and principles using critical judgment. Such judgment is built up through intelligent critical practice, when one performance is modified by previous performances.

In the process of learning how to teach, some valuable technical knowledge can justifiably be passed on at college prior to practice; for instance, certain general rules of procedure, management techniques and possible plans of action. Nevertheless, Ryle makes the significant point that 'we learn *how* by practice, schooled indeed by criticism and example, but often quite unaided by any lessons in the theory'.[14] This implies that formal explanations of the principles of teaching are likely to have far less effect on students than periods of critical practice accompanied by theoretical advice from college staff and teachers in a practical context. Informed and guided school experience is central to the development of the practical knowledge required in teaching, but both the judgment and style implicit in good teaching may be best acquired by students being in continuous contact with a competent performer. There is much to be said for the adoption of a 'teacher-tutor' system in schools, because as a student needs to identify himself with some model, it is preferable that the exemplar be an expert, so that there is less chance of reverting to some unsatisfactory earlier model.[15] In such a system the essential interaction between the theoretical and practical knowledge could be drawn out by the teacher as well as by the college tutor. The supervisory role of the teacher-tutor would have to be made explicit, and he would need to be specially trained to assist in the planning of student programmes, to guide students in the evaluation of their work and to help them develop the ability to make informed practical judgments in different teaching situations. Not only would students benefit from such a scheme, but it would also enable a closer relationship between schools and colleges to be established, and encourage teachers to reflect critically on both the nature of their task and on the rationale underlying the many practical and theoretical activities that take place in a classroom.

This closer link between schools and colleges must assume central importance in the future, not only in the course of initial training but also during the probationary year and subsequent in-service training. At present, as Professor Perry demonstrates,[16] there is a tendency for some schools to *retrain* probationary teachers along lines which conflict with the principles underlying initial training; in fact, there is a gulf in communication between the different sectors engaged in the training of teachers. Perry crystallizes the difference between initial training and school retraining when he states that 'whereas the initial system attempts to cultivate a self-critical appraisal of teaching, the school retraining . . . regards teaching as a static and routine situation for which permanent solutions in terms of teaching method are applicable'.[17] If this state of affairs is to improve, initial training, probationary year and in-service training must be viewed as a continuum based on a body of rationally determined and agreed principles. This is essential if we are to achieve a cohesive knowledge-based profession. Implicit in this idea of professionalism is the need for teachers to gain the authority, autonomy and breadth of understanding which will enable them to make informed professional judgments. This strengthens the case for student-teachers to receive a general education which must be gained through academic study conceived within a professional frame of reference.

The objectives of the college of education curriculum

In the light of the preceding anlysis of academic and professional studies are we any nearer to formulating the general principles that might guide the planning of a college curriculum? Can we make explicit a set of objectives that are both logically consistent and that reflect the growing professional, technological and social demands confronting the teacher in schools? I would suggest that the following objectives are central to any teacher education programme, but in order to be effective guides for action they would have to be reformulated in more specific operational terms and then applied to the relevant components of the college curriculum.

(a) To develop, through academic study, an understanding of those areas of knowledge which have professional significance. Such study would involve:

(i) Grasping the central facts, concepts and principles of the particular disciplines that the student intends to teach.

(ii) Understanding the specific organization or distinctive structure of key concepts within each area of knowledge.

(iii) Learning how to use the different methods of enquiry and verification procedures within each form of thought.

(iv) Gaining a broad perspective through grasping the conceptual interconnections between different modes of understanding

(v) Developing such qualities of mind as logical and critical thought, creative imagination, judgment, rationality and autonomy in relation to each area of knowledge.

(b) To develop, through academic study, an understanding of educational theory which will inform professional judgments and actions. In this area of the curriculum the emphasis would be on:

(i) The formulation of rational principles acquired through the objective study of the contributory disciplines.

(ii) The examination of the principles underlying curriculum planning and evaluation in schools.

(iii) Understanding the factors that affect the development of children.

(iv) Acquiring a sensitive awareness of the dynamic relationship between school and society.

(v) Building up the knowledge and attitudes that will enable students to understand the demands and pressures arising from our advanced industrial and pluralistic society.

(vi) Gaining an understanding of the diffuse nature of the teacher's role.

(vii) Developing an occupational consciousness by sharpening the students' political, economic and sociological insights.

(viii) Fostering a flexibility of mind and a constructive, critical attitude towards educational innovation, which will enable students to evaluate the changing conception of teaching and research findings in the light of rational criteria.

(c) To develop, through training and practical experience, the technical skills necessary for the achievement of professional competence in teaching. This area of activity would stress:

(i) The acquisition of a range of skills focused on teaching methods, appropriate learning experiences and motivation in the classroom, management and organizational expertise, evaluation procedures and record keeping.

(ii) The development of the student's critical skill, judgment and powers of reflection, thus giving him the ability to modify his performances in the light of growing experience.

(d) To develop, through academic and professional study, a knowledge of the relationship between the logical and psychological aspects of learning and teaching at the different stages of children's development.

In conclusion, I would stress that the overall aim of a college curriculum is to produce teachers who, by virtue of their education and training, are sensitive, self-confident, self-critical and adaptable persons with the ability to work as a link in a complex differentiated teaching force. If this aim were realized, perhaps we could achieve a knowledge-based profession, thus raising the academic and professional standards of the teacher, which would enhance his status in society and benefit future generations of children.

References

1 Ministry of Education (1957), *The Training of Teachers*, Pamphlet No. 34, London, H.M.S.O., p. 6.
2 University of London Institute of Education (1951–2), *Regulations and Syllabuses for the Teacher's Certificate*, pp. 7–8, para. 8.
3 University of London Institute of Education (1963–4), *Regulations and Syllabuses for the Teacher's Certificate*, p. 10, para. 8.
4 Hirst, P. H. (1965), 'Liberal education and the nature of knowledge' in Archambault, R. D., ed., *Philosophical Analysis and Education*, Routledge & Kegan Paul, pp. 116–21.
5 Higginbotham, P. J. (1969), 'The concepts of professional and academic studies in relation to courses in institutes of higher education (particularly colleges of education)' in *British Journal of Educational Studies*, Vol. XVII, No. 1, February, p. 57.
6 Bloom, B. S. (1965), *Taxonomy of Educational Objectives*, Vol. 1, 'Cognitive domain', New York, D. McKay, p. 63.
7 Bruner, J. S. (1960), *The Process of Education*, Cambridge, Harvard University Press, p. 23.
8 Bruner, J. S. (1962), *On Knowing*, Cambridge, Harvard University Press, p. 120.
9 Bloom, B. S., ed., *ibid.*, pp. 72–3.
10 Taylor, W. (1964), 'The organization of educational studies', in *Education for Teaching*, No. 65, November, p. 29.
11 Peters, R. S., 'Comments on a discipline of education', in Walton, J. and Kuethe, J. L. (1963), eds., *The Discipline of Education*, Wisconsin Press, p. 17.
12 Hirst, P. H. (1966), 'Educational theory', in Tibble, J. W., ed., *The Study of Education*, Routledge & Kegan Paul, pp. 47–57.

13 Ryle, G. (1963), *The Concept of Mind*, Peregrine, p. 42.
14 Ryle, G., *ibid.*, p. 41.
15 For instance see:
   Baker, J. R. (1967), 'A teacher co-tutor scheme', in *Education for Teaching*, No. 73, pp. 25–30.
   Caspari, I. E., and Eggleston, J. (1965), 'A new approach to supervision of teaching practice', in *Education for Teaching*, No. 68, November, pp. 42–52.
   Hollins, T. H. B. (1969), *Another Look at Teacher Training*, Leeds University Press, pp. 18–19.
   Taylor, W. (1969), *Society and the Education of Teachers*, Faber, pp. 163–4.
   Tibble, J. W. (1966), 'Practical work training in the education of teachers', in *Education for Teaching*, No. 70, May, pp. 49–54.
16 Perry, L. R. (1969), 'Training', in *Education for Teaching*, No. 79, p. 6.
17 Ibid., p. 8.

Four	**The Study of Education in the Colleges.**
Peter Chambers	**Harking Back!**

An education lecturer trying to estimate the future of educational studies in colleges of education in the present climate of explosive change and uncertain objectives can be likened only to Leacock's Lord Ronald, who 'flung himself upon his horse and rode madly off in all directions'.[1] As the historical survey in chapter one reveals, he can take guide from the past which draws from the tradition of the skilled practising teacher as exemplified by the Master of Method. He can find advocates for this approach today recommending departments of 'Applied Education' for the colleges of the future. Similarly he can look back on theory that owes more to the university than the classroom, when the university teachers developed the study of the philosophy, history and psychology of education and the Board of Education examined the professional training of students in the Day Training Colleges.[2] The consequence of this approach can also be seen today, and as a prospect for the future, in those colleges which have created 'academic' education departments, or even done away with them to create departments of psychology and the like. The analysis of the structure of colleges in chapter three draws attention to two other competing and often conflicting traditions: the unified study of education as opposed to the separate study of the foundation disciplines. Both can find venerable antecedents as Tibble[3] has shown in *The Study of Education*. Looking to the future, the development of curriculum theory inherits the mantle of the first, while the development of B.Ed. courses gives impetus to the second.[4] The various components of the education course have vied for precedence in the past. The once supreme repository of academic respectability, the history of education, has been overtaken by sociology. Psychology and philosophy have also had their day. Now history and philosophy are fighting back and their professional societies flourish.[5] It would be a brave man who would forecast which will be the bandwagon of the 1980s. Examination of the back numbers of the *Bulletin of Education* and *Education for Teaching* reveal a similarly rich, intricate and interwoven set of traditions about almost every other aspect of the education course. It has been central and peripheral; integrative and exclusive. It has been the responsibility of the principal and it has been conducted by outsiders. Nevertheless, the education lecturer has always been there[6] and the combination of method work and the theory of education has usually characterized his work[7]. A confused past, a major source of role diffusion and a complex role set make conflict inherent in such a lecturer's role performance,[8] and it is on the basis of this conflict that on-going behaviour will be formed. Ambivalence about academic or pedagogical priorities will colour the future of educational studies. What is certain is that the subject, education, will try to do both, that is, give coherence to the personal education of students and contribute to their professional training as teachers. In so doing, it may mean riding off in a diversity of directions.

Here and now

Whereas no monolithic theories of education or unified ideal types can be described, there are a number of common elements in education courses that indicate some similar patterns. *The Study of Education*, already referred to, indicates how the omni-competent, autonomous education tutor is losing out to the specialist in a foundation discipline. T. H. Huxley complained in 1884 that 'the amount of scientific literature that is produced . . . is something stupendous. I feel I want to have the whole thing stopped for a time to enable one to read up a little of it'.[9] The 158 references to educational writings published since 1960, which grace 'the Study of Education', indicate that the problem is still as great and the tutor's answer has often been to concentrate on single areas. If the urge to publish cannot be stopped, at least certain areas can be ignored! The result has been to see a change in the personnel of departments and in the interpretation of their roles. Mother hens may still abound but the rapid expansion of the 1960s saw them being outnumbered by specialist tutors. Less and less are whole groups of students being carefully tended by the same tutor for the entire course. They are more likely to follow a common theoretical course in psychology, sociology, philosophy and history taught by a number of specialists in related disciplines, which is applied or integrated by their education tutor. This has produced a number of high-level theoretical courses which have stimulated and challenged the students and which offer growth points for the development of educational studies. It has also ensured a genuine attempt to show their relevance and allowed the professionally orientated tutor to indicate another area of growth, that of curriculum studies. This attempt to get the best of both worlds was challenged by the increasing interest of outside specialists. The B.P.S./A.T.C.D.E. Report of 1962,[10] the surveys conducted by the A.T.C.D.E. Sociology Section in 1968[11] and 1969[12] have cast major doubts on the function of quasi-specialists. The introduction of B.Ed. courses increased these doubts still more. As a result, very few education lecturers feel competent to expound their theory except within the safety of a single academic discipline. In the context of the knowledge explosion, this has produced another current trend, the greater compartmentalization of professional and academic work. In some cases this has meant the rationalization of staff with its divisive consequences and, in others, the segregating of courses, with its problems of coherence for the students. The tendency, on the one hand, for some lecturers to assume greater and greater responsibility for professional courses and teaching practices and, on the other, for some to shy away from their responsibilities in these areas has added to the confusion. It has hardly provided that 'distinctive professional commitment' shared by staff and students that Renshaw suggests in the preceding chapter represents the unique character of colleges of education. Rather does it emphasize the alleged dichotomy between professional and academic courses. These trends are mirrored in two other critical influences that affect the work of education departments, the students themselves[13] and the teaching profession.[14] Whereas the academic sociologists or psychologists are able to maintain their own status needs by adhering to their subject expertise, both students and teachers are clamouring for greater relevance in their training courses and more expert supervision of teaching practice. The future answers to these dilemmas will be structural as well as curricular, but the immediate consequence has been to see a development of the curriculum courses in the education tutor's work and a concern for professional objectives in the teaching of the foundation disciplines.[15] Thus, gradually, there is a move back to the kind of reasoning in which psychology was justified because of its contribution to the understanding of classroom teaching, philosophy because of its function in clarifying teaching aims, sociology because of its part in developing awareness of social pressures on a teacher's work and history because of its insights into traditional restraints on the practice of teaching. This movement to an academically justifiable professionally orientated education course is admirably summarized in the objectives of educational theory described in the previous chapter. The only reservations are related to the time available to achieve them and the organization of the curriculum to make them precise. The formulation of such objectives and the kind of teaching necessary to fulfil them demands feedback and evaluation.[16] It has led to a further professionalization of the theory courses and the recognition that rigour need not be lost. The specialist movement was almost certainly necessary to change educational theory from 'mush' to 'mesh',[17] but on its own it would have remained sterile and arid. The future demands a new level of integration in which the rigorous and disciplined pursuit of some specialism acts as a focus for integrating a student's understanding of the theoretical bases of his work as a teacher.

Curriculum theory
Some appreciation of curriculum theory is necessary for a student, or for that matter a tutor, to understand how his discipline can contribute to the process of professional education. Whether the curriculum is considered in terms of content or as a guide for teaching, some estimate of learning outcomes and their evaluation is a prerequisite[18] of necessity, curriculum theory requires the formulation of objectives, the examination of restraints on their achievement, the enacting of certain instructional procedures and the systematic evaluation of these interrelated elements.[19] Consequently, education lecturers have had to examine their aims and methods in terms of their intended learning outcomes.[20] Sifting through the confused maze of tradition and practice described in this chapter, it becomes clear that any consensus about objectives would centre on the need to provide a balanced course appropriate to institutions of higher education with a particular concern for the training of teachers. It would have to be an academic course designed to challenge a student, further his personal education and give him insights into his own development; and also a course designed specifically to strengthen his work as a teacher, equipping him with skills, information, and focused attitudes to children and schools.[21] From the first priority, the outcomes might be thought of in terms of the capacity

F

to make dispassionate judgments, to pursue intellectual activity with rigour and single-mindedness, and to recognize the value of distinguished scholarship.[22] From the second, the student might be expected to assess the contribution of educational theory to the process of helping a new generation to develop those forms of understanding and awareness which make up being 'educated'.[23] The inherent conflict will lead to tension and problems of priorities and the balance may change, but there will be a constant reminder of the need to illustrate theory and principle in practical ways and to support practice with good theory. It is usually agreed that the first requirement for personal education is study in depth. This is unlikely to be provided in a three-year course devoted to a proliferation of academic, professional and practical studies. Even the increasing rigour with which the foundation disciplines have been pursued has done little more than scratch the surface. Courses have been described as introductory, 'An Introduction to the Sociology of Education' etc., but the snag has so often been in the past that they have never got past the introduction to the course itself! It would seem imperative then that the future of educational studies will see increasing specialization. It cannot, however, be at the expense of pedagogical relevance. Awareness of teaching skills, learning situations and curricular consequences require a broader basis of understanding. Thus the opportunity for studying a discipline in depth must be provided within a framework of curriculum theory. It may well be that the best model to explain this approach is that of the spiral curriculum.[24] The student follows a broad base of curriculum studies at the start of his course, visiting schools, observing children and learning skills. The broad contribution of educational theory is presented through the disciplines in implicit rather than explicit ways. As he continues, the disciplines are identified and introduced so that his course may end in a detailed study, in depth, of one such discipline, which he has chosen in the light of his interests as the course went on. Such an approach would require teams of specialists working in close contact with the schools whose objectives would be first to equip a student in such a way that he could decide which discipline would be most use to him, and, second, to take him into the unique insights that his chosen discipline offers in the study of education. An examination of the foundation disciplines will illustrate possible objectives of this final study in depth. The order of presentation is arbitrary.

The history of education

The intending historian will have seen the importance of child development and learning theory, he will have made decisions about teaching practice under the influence of social and institutional pressures and he will have begun to appreciate that the ways in which he thinks about his work have been shaped by the patterns of his value judgments. The objectives of his final study will be to integrate these areas around the perspectives of history. As Collier[25] suggests this is likely to be 'a habit of intellectual operation' in which the historian has to judge the importance of evidence and its relevance to the question at issue. In curriculum terms, this may mean an appreciation of the traditional perspectives of educational practice, indicating the constraints imposed and the opportunities offered, and these may be sociological, psychological or philosophical. It may mean an analysis of the educational possibilities inherent within systems and schools. It will certainly mean an understanding of the influence of the interaction of the past with the present in whatever form of educational practice the student chooses to consider. It should lead to the promoting of change, for such a perspective could lead to a fostering of awareness of how educational changes have come about. The realization that things have not always been done in their present ways has often exploded a belief in the necessity of continuing to to do them so! This would be related to the content of courses, to teaching, to organization and to assessment. It could also develop an understanding of the relationship between the social structure and the process of education. It is easy to dismiss this as sociology with hindsight, but it would be foolish to deny the importance of this perspective to the teacher and the real contribution the historian can make. Better historians will be able to develop this process still further, but there can be little doubt that such a course would provide both the rigour and concentration esteemed by the academic and the broad professional insights required of the practising teacher.

The philosophy of education

The philosopher, too, after an introduction to the epistemologies of history, psychology and sociology would have begun to focus his attentions on the importance of theory and the contribution of 'second order' philosophy. As a philosopher, he will be beginning to sort out the conceptual issues involved in educational policy and practice.[26] His first objective will be to assist the process of clarifying his own thinking about the objectives of his teaching. Students' presentations of aims in lesson preparation have stood in great need of 'semantic hygiene' for many years. The contribution of philosophy to educational theory[27] along these lines and at many levels could mean a major breakthrough not only in determining criteria for curriculum decision-making but also in establishing much more precise forms of evaluating instructional effectiveness. This would require a full appreciation of the nature of evidence used and its epistemological sources. In particular, it might well serve as a synthesis of the related contributions to professional training of sociology or psychology. Closely related to the clarification of objectives would be attempts to make more precise a student's understanding of the value judgments implicit in his educational practices. Analysis of such values and their relationship to the self or society; development of their educational implications in psychological or sociological terms; and conceptualization of the assumptions on which they are based represent some of the most exacting intellectual pursuits and also some of the most utilitarian professional skills. The reliance on intuition in teaching may serve those who learn from sitting with Nellie, they are hardly sufficient for coping with the rate of change endemic in English education. Both Professor Hirst and Professor Peters have taken this argument further, but one other contribution of the philosopher to professional practice deserves a mention, namely, the ways in which it serves to make manifest to the teacher the consequences of his actions in undertaking different kinds of teaching. In terms of developing techniques of evaluation and as ways of ordering knowledge, the philosopher's concern for the systematization of intended learning outcomes is of the utmost importance. Again it is easy to indicate how such an approach has both relevance and rigour.

Educational psychology

The student will have been exposed to more educational psychology than almost any other strand of the education course in the early school-based parts of his course. He will have learnt the value of the systematic observation of children, the importance of developmental studies, the contribution of learning theories, the influence of personality on education and the effects of individual differences. He will have seen this against other sociological and traditional influences. To this practical and active approach he must bring the rigorous, empirical perspective of the social scientist. As Taylor[28] insists, 'psychology is a science and as such is governed by a morality or code of rules which calls for the empirical verification of its proportions.'

In his concentrated study, he will bring this regard for the scientific method to re-examining the early curriculum course as described above. For example, he could focus on developing an understanding of how children learn in ways that will bear the scrutiny of careful empirical research. He will be able to develop experimental situations in which the learning variables can be isolated so that he might accurately discriminate between significant elements and those which are there by chance. Morris' appeal for relevance[29] underlines the need for psychological thought of this kind to be applied to education. In the light of the vast areas of psychological research, the criteria for selecting content become crucial. It has already been suggested that learning theory is of the utmost importance. To go further, it could well become the central focus of the student's ultimate study. He would perceive how growth and development affect learning, how the various theories have evolved and how they have affected curriculum practice and how current research is shaping the approaches to the organization of learning. He will be able to bring psychological insights to his understanding of educational technology. To this, he must add some appreciation of how the interaction of people gives direction to teaching and learning and also imposes restraints and limitations upon it. Perhaps his most important contribution will be to help promote and develop evaluation devices so that he can measure the effectiveness of his own, and others', organization of learning experiences. The rigour of focused psychological study of this kind will be very demanding on many students, but if it draws out of adequate initial courses in curriculum study, it will have the relevance that motivates students today and should continue to do so in the future. It will have a further professional advantage in that the promotion of the sophisticated use of psychological measurement and its application in the classroom may ensure fuller co-operation with other social and welfare agencies and, if carried out successfully, will free the teacher from dependence on the outside interpretation of data in ways consistent with the professional status so highly esteemed by teachers.

The sociology of education

The sociologist will have had the benefits of personality study, learning theory and language development from his introduction to psychology. He will know some history and have drawn from the contact with philosophers. This is an admirable basis for understanding the results of a scientific study of society[30] and applying this knowledge of 'social realities' to education. The professional objectives behind an intensive study of the sociology of education fall into two main categories, both concerned with helping a student systematize his perceptions of social forces. The first is concerned with social structure and society; the second is concerned with institutional and group processes which affect his work in the classroom. They can gain cohesion from analysis of role. As Eggleston[31] indicates 'It is in the analysis of role that the social scientist's study of social structures, organizations and culture patterns can most clearly be seen to have real relevance to human behaviour.' Thus central to a student's main study would be careful analysis of the concept of teacher's role, which would aim to help him make maximum use of himself as a social agent in the learning process. This would call for detailed study of the institution of education, the social structure of schools, their social systems and their organizations.

It would enable him to organize his teaching so as to take into account the varied social influences on learning. This would involve a deep understanding of the two ubiquitous social processes of socialization and stratification and their cumulative effect on educability. With the benefits of the study of organizational theory, a student would be helped to develop an awareness of how institutional pressures set limits on his implementation of the curriculum and his analysis of how schools function would give fresh insights into problems of authority, acculturation and relative deprivation. Partly because of the writer's predilections, it seems almost more obvious in sociology than elsewhere that these insights can only come from study in depth. It needs a good sociologist to appreciate the sociology of the curriculum; the amateur is much more susceptible to the distortions of selective perception and is less likely to discriminate between fact and value. At the same time, the pedagogical implications of Goffman or Etzioni need an educationalist to synthesize them in a study of the curriculum.

This attempt to show how the disciplines can contribute to curriculum theory has, of necessity, been a 'Cook's Tour', and any specialist worth his salt can extend the argument further. It is hoped that he will, for it merely strengthens the case and one of the purposes of this chapter is to suggest ways in which the debate can be projected into the future.

Having stated the objectives of the disciplines in curricular terms, it becomes clear that the methods of teaching and evaluating them can be limited to two criteria: academic excellence as measured by the existing criteria of a recognized discipline, and the capacity to apply the perspectives to either teaching or the curriculum. The first is already well established but the critical appraisal initiated by the second suggests that this must be one of the major questions that will be posed about educational studies in the next ten years.

In summary, then, one major line that education is likely to follow in the future is a spiral course in which the professional aspects of what used to be the education course are integrated in a multi-disciplinary introduction to the curriculum of schools.[32] In so doing, the course will attempt to answer the question: what should we intend our pupils to learn? It should offer a consistent scheme for planning, implementing and evaluating educational objectives. To take it beyond the immediate and the pragmatic and establish sound theoretical principles for future flexibility, it will need to identify the part played by the different foundation disciplines and introduce these to the student. With this knowledge, the student should then be able to judge the most appropriate area in which to specialize and pursue his final curriculum studies in depth within the framework of an academic discipline. There is no reason to suggest that any such course will be any less balanced than the existing multi-disciplined one. Indeed, it would seem more probable that its organization would not only provide the professional relevance necessary to give focus to the disciplines but also provide the 'rationality, autonomy, judgment, imagination, critical and logical thought' that Renshaw has rightly indicated to be the marks of personal development.

And then what?

No mention has been made of other lines of enquiry. The delicate
problems of relationships with the rest of the course, the place
of educational studies within monotechnic or polytechnic institutions, the function of school practice, the increasingly close
relationships with schools and the general integration of training
courses are all dealt with in other chapters. The developments
forecast in this chapter would fit most existing patterns of training
and are sufficiently flexible to provide an acceptable nucleus of
professional training for any institution likely to appear in the
foreseeable future. Indeed it is likely that such a course would
provide an integrative approach for those developments of a
polytechnic nature in which the main subject and the pedagogical
courses proper are offered alongside educational theory.[33] It
would also provide the necessary basis for curriculum innovation
and development as envisaged by Joselin[34] in the context of a
technological university and by Michael Young in terms of social
engineering through education.[35] At the present, departments of
education have sometimes been squeezed into Cinderella status
by their unique position in the college course. The enormous
demands presented by the wide objectives assumed by the poly-
math tradition have probably been too great. Teaching the entire
student population too much has been a notable challenge in
which much has been achieved but the remorseless logic of
numbers has wearied the education departments on the way. The
focus provided by specialized curriculum studies in the present
state of change can provide a fresh impetus. The unifying central
core that education once held in the college course was lost when
education tutors split into the professionals and the academic.
Those who invested status and prestige in their craft 'mystery'
were unable to give the lead to others in developing the professional
side of their work. The others who declared themselves to be
sociologists or philosophers and treated professional work as
peripheral flew in the face of a powerful tradition. Under the
pressures of expansion and in the face of criticism they have found
a common bond in curriculum study. To do this well required
exploration of subject boundaries, redefining of objectives and
reorganization of functions. The sociologists, psychologists,
philosophers, historians and methodologists in the education
department have come together as a team to replace the principal's

lecture and the Master of Method's demonstration as the unifying element in the professional preparation of teachers. The future surely holds a prospect of similar groupings, which will draw from the main subject courses. In addition it will also provide opportunities for establishing closer connections with the schools both in the lower coils of the spiral and through the curricular implications of the depth study of the discipline. If partnership in teams has any meaning within the college walls, in the future, it will gain new meanings for the development of innovatory theory through partnership with the schools. Whatever the present stage of discussion in the interrelationship of theory and practice, if the study of education is to survive it must establish a genuinely conjugal relationship. Then it will not only survive but flourish as the central focus of teacher education.

The debate will continue and role conflict will clamour at the lecturer in education of the future, but as this chapter has tried to show, conflict is functional in ensuring change.

References

1 Leacock, S., 'Gertrude the Governess,' *Nonsense Novels*, Lane, 1926.
2 Jones, L. G. E., *The Training of Teachers in England and Wales*, Milford, 1924.
3 Tibble, J. W. (1966), ed., *The Study of Education*, Routledge & Kegan Paul.
4 Wadd, K. (1969), 'A source of conflict in colleges of education', in *Education for Teaching*, No. 78, Spring.
5 See for example *The History of Education Society Bulletin*, No. 4, Autumn, 1969.
6 Evans, L. M. (1969), 'The role of the education lecturer in the college of education', in *Education for Teaching*, No. 80, Autumn.
7 Taylor, W. (1964), 'The organization of educational studies', in *Education for Teaching*, No. 65, November.
8 Merton, R. K. (1957), 'The role-set: problems in sociological theory', in *British Journal of Sociology*, Vol. VII, No. 2.
9 Huxley, T. H. (1884), *Royal Commission on Technical Instruction*, 1884.
10 B.P.S./A.T.C.D.E. Report (1962), *Teaching Educational Psychology in Training Colleges*, August.
11 Ellis, D., McCready, D., and Morgan, C. (1969), 'Sociology main courses in colleges of education', in *Sociology in the Education of Teachers*, A.T.C.D.E.
12 Chambers, P. (1969), 'The sociology of education in education courses: an analysis', in *Report of the Joint DES/ATCDE Conference on the Sociology of Education in Colleges of Education*, D.E.S.

13 N.U.S. (1966), *Report on the Three Year Course in Colleges of Education.*

14 Kent Education Committee (1966), *The Three Year Course of Teacher Training.*

15 Kerr, J. F. (1968), ed., *Changing the Curriculum*, University of London Press.

16 Stones, E. (1970), ed., *Towards Evaluation*, University of Birmingham.

17 Taylor, W., *op. cit.*

18 Brailsford, D., and Taylor, P. H., eds., *An Introduction to Curriculum Studies* (in press).

19 Stones, E., *op. cit.*

20 Boucher, L., and Starkey, F. C. (1970), 'Curriculum development and evaluation in education courses', in *Education for Teaching*, No. 82, Summer.

21 Taylor, W. (1969), *Society and the Education of Teachers*, Faber.

22 Niblett, W. R. (1967), 'Education: professional concern or academic discipline?' in *The Education and Training of Teachers*, D.E.S.

23 Peters, R. S. (1963), 'Education as a specific training for teachers', in *The Education and Training of Teachers*, D.E.S.

24 Renshaw, P. (1968), 'A re-appraisal of the college of education curriculum', in *Education for Teaching*, No. 75, Spring.

25 Collier, K. G. (1968), *New Dimensions in Higher Education*, Longmans.

26 Peters, R. S. (1966), in *The Study of Education*, ed. Tibble, J. W., Routledge & Kegan Paul.

27 Hirst, P. H. (1966), in *The Study of Education*, ed. Tibble, J. W., Routledge & Kegan Paul.

28 Taylor, P. H. (1968), in *Changing the Curriculum*, ed. Kerr, J. F., University of London Press.

29 Morris, B. (1966), in *The Study of Education*, ed. Tibble, J. W., Routledge & Kegan Paul.

30 Neustadt, I. (1965), *Teaching Sociology*, Leicester University Press.

31 Eggleston, S. J. (1969), ed., *Paedagogica Europaea*, Vol. V.

32 Whitfield, R. C. (1970), 'The core of a study of education for teachers', in *Education for Teaching*, No. 82, Summer.

33 Ross, A. (1970), *Curriculum and the initial training of a teacher*, D.E.S./A.T.C.D.E. Conference, July.

34 Joselin, A. (1969), *Education and the Technological University*, University of Aston in Birmingham.

35 Young, M. (1965), *Innovation and Research in Education*, Routledge & Kegan Paul.

Five	**Main**
	Subject
T. W. Eason	**Courses**

In his letter of February 1970, calling for enquiries to be made by the Area Training Organizations into 'teacher education', the Secretary of State for Education and Science (Mr Edward Short) named 'the structure of the course' in colleges of education as the first of four areas on which concern had been expressed.

Well he might. On this subject there is a great deal of obscurity and ambiguity. Some educational reforms start with a manifesto, and thereafter the question is simply to see how far the expressed aims have been carried out. Such a reformer, like Luther nailing his ninety-five theses to the great door of the church in Wittenberg, or the American settlers issuing their ringing Declaration, sets out unequivocally and precisely the lines of policy. The rationale is there from the beginning.

Such movements are rare at any time, whether in education or in politics generally. Most of the time changes are made piecemeal by busy people subject to all the constraints of immediate problems, and only retrospectively can the general pattern of development be discerned. The colleges of education, like the schools, have changed tremendously and continuously over twenty years, which is barely half the working life of a professional man! As a result, the contemporary 'training college' must be almost as unfamiliar in structure and organization to students only a few years out, as today's primary school is at first to mature trainee teachers or middle-aged parents. What is badly needed today by those working both in schools and in the teacher education service is a rationale to put the changes in structure, recruitment and purpose of the last two decades into perspective, and provide a guideline for the future.

Very much at the centre of this is the need for a rationale covering the place of the 'main' or 'subject' courses in relation to the overall purpose and functioning of the college. Everyone knows these 'main courses' to be descendants in some sense of the pre-war training college subject courses. Most teachers will know there was, until twenty years ago, a nationally specified list of these (group A: English, history, geography, mathematics, science, French . . .; group B: music, drawing, handwork, gardening; for women housecraft or needlework) any student being required to take four or five, chosen out of the dozen; where today the student chooses one, or perhaps two, out of a longer, more variegated and ambitious list which may include philosophy, social work, or evolution and prehistory, and which varies substantially from college to college. The feeling is abroad that perhaps the vocational usefulness for a primary teacher of a programme with one such 'main course' is less obvious than its possible academic prestige, particularly if the same course is also available towards a Bachelor of Education degree.

The very name of 'main course'[1] is itself odd, if one reflects that it is 'education' which is the common course element for all 'education students', and that *prima facie* the paring of the demand for a wide range of work in school subjects means that subject courses may involve *relatively* few students and *relatively* small classes. The term 'main course', originally correlative to the now obsolescent term 'subsidiary', has come to stand in opposition to 'education course' and to reinforce the unintended implication that for the college concerned academic subject studies are the main thing, the study of education and professional training are ancillary.

Tension between the demands (staffing, timetabling) of main courses and education courses has in fact been endemic, and this purely historical accident of a name has done nothing to clarify a confused situation. For a plain illustration of the need for a new rationale of the main course, look at the D.E.S. Report on Education number 49, published in 1968 for general public information, on *Colleges of Education*. The point about such a document is precisely that it is representative; it presents the structure of the training courses as they would be generally viewed at the time by responsible official opinion.

On the general curricular structure of the college of education the Report states, 'In the college course, the personal higher education of the student is carried out concurrently with his professional training as a teacher'—thus giving a particular meaning to the word 'concurrent'—and goes on: 'For the former [his personal higher education] the student studies in depth one or two "main subjects" ', on the professional side however undertaking 'studies in the philosophy, psychology, and sociology of education and in the *teaching* [my italics] of a range of subjects'.

The lines I have quoted are the obviously crucial passage of justification for college 'main courses', the concern of this chapter. But the inadequacy of some other assumptions made (and hence of the procedures they might be held to justify) are all relevant to the present difficulty in understanding the role of the 'main courses' in teacher education. This is because, in this formulation, the main academic study is presented as divorced from the professional side, instead of being perceived as each student's central and deepest engagement with the curriculum; as a result, his 'education' studies are reduced to an anodyne collection of 'philosophy, psychology, and sociology'; and any involvement with curriculum is reduced to mere methodology of a range of subjects. Nothing wrong with methodology. It is important, and the proper concern equally of college staff working in subject and education departments. But, for a document issued in the late sixties, this is an inadequate and misleading conception of the kind of bite education and subject courses must direct towards curriculum.

What is out of date in that formulation is that it (a) reduces the study of education to an agglomeration of psychology, sociology, and so on, disciplines which are properly seen as 'contributory' to the study of education rather than constitutive of it; (b) limits any concern professional studies may have with curriculum to a few aspects of subject methodology; and (c) identifies each student's 'main course' as a factor in his personal education but not as a main element in his professional education. None of this will do.

What is right about the formulation lies in its stress on the fact that the main courses (along, one has to add, with all the other activities comprising the curriculum of the college) are concerned with the personal *education* of each student, and that this education is concurrent with professional apprenticeship, not only in the weak sense of going on simultaneously, but in the strong sense that each reinforces and acts as a channel for the other.

It is a logical feature of teaching, as a profession, unlike dentistry or civil engineering, that general education not only informs and extends professional competence, but is part of it. A man 'must himself be *educated* before he can educate others'. This dictum of Derwent Coleridge's dates from the first foundation of an elementary training college, and it is still valid at a time when there is a tendency to confuse education with socialization, therapy, social work, and other useful processes.[2] But in itself this formulation of Coleridge's is too general to serve.

In evaluating courses of preparation for any profession, and not merely for teaching—the work of a doctor, lawyer, architect, librarian, or nurse—the case for professional education rather than vocational training rests on the non-routine character of the skills involved in carrying out the professional tasks. To the extent that judgment, seeing unexpected applications or devising new approaches in the light of fundamental theory is continuously needed, to that extent there is a demand for professional education.

The general distinction is clear, but determination of the boundary in individual cases need not be easy. For all Coleridge's high aims, the elementary teacher in Victorian times and till quite recently tended to be regarded as a higher tradesman, and his training to be cut-and-dried and specific. Only twenty years ago, at the beginning of our current period, the colleges were facing the change from their role of providing teachers for elementary schools. Even in more recent years the need for professional levels of insight among teachers of 'young children' was more readily grasped in relation to psychological development or understanding of social background, than in relation to (say) the infant school curriculum.

Certainly the old 'ordinary' amd 'advanced' college subject courses were easily seen as providing cut-and-dried 'lesson content' rather than as personal education contributing to the professional autonomy and responsibility of the elementary teacher. A polarization of views came into the open as late as 1925—at about the time when the Hadow Committee was attempting to lever the higher elementary school into the twentieth century—in a form surprisingly close and relevant to the issue as it confronts us today again. A report published in that year on the training of teachers for public elementary schools[3] outlines many of the positions taken up again later, and is still controversial. The 'double function' of the college, completing the academic education of the teacher and beginning direct preparation for his teaching service, involved 'a certain undesirable distraction of aim', and particularly 'a bias towards the academic work', diminishing unnecessarily the practical effectiveness of the training. Two solutions were proposed, mutually contradictory. A radical dissenting paper argued flatly for the college to be relieved of any need to concern itself with what we should now call 'main courses' at all.

We want places of professional training, content to leave
academic studies to academic institutions, and to devote
themselves with a single eye to the important task of teaching
recruits how to teach. . . . And we are sure that we shall not
get it, if each student is required to study one or two
academic subjects. . . and if the colleges are to be staffed
so as to be able to provide instruction to a high pitch in the
subjects taken.

This proposal, 'that all college courses should be post-academic',
has its own resemblance to a current idea that colleges should
offer a short 'post-academic' professional course, to follow after
a two-year liberal arts (or liberal arts and science) course taken
without professional commitment. As against this, the proposals
of the majority have a different, though also a modern, ring.
The college course should, it was thought, 'become more professional in character and aim'; and 'the academic work . . . should
be undertaken primarily as a means to professional skill.' Subjects
'should be looked at as material for studying teaching-method'.
As if to resile from the narrowness implied in that sentence,
however, larger views were put forward. 'We desire to see the
course more professional, but not less educative.' The student,
in his subject courses, would not be concerned with getting up
more facts, the learning of which would have ceased to be the
main consideration in his academic studies; at this stage his
concern would be with 'the study of principles, thinking about
subjects, reconsidering them', and this with special reference to
'the principles underlying them and to those aspects of them and
ways of presenting them which are likely to appeal . . . to children'.
Some of the language here betrays the date—we should now
speak of 'the logical and psychological aspects of learning' to
express the general import of the second quoted passage—but
mutatis mutandis the committee of 1925 was putting forward
proposals closer in spirit to the present direction being taken in
the colleges of education than one might expect, and offered a
better rationale for such a policy than has lately been current.

The sense of *déjà vu* is all the greater when one mentions
further recommendations that reappear substantially in the
McNair Report and underlie, with one exception to be noted
later, the present certificate course structure: one subject (excep-
tionally two) to be taken by each student 'to as high a pitch as

can be attained', and an examination in this 'main course' to be the only explicit test of academic knowledge as such during the course. There would also be a test (practical or otherwise) 'devised to examine the proficiency of students with regard to the teaching of all the ordinary subjects . . .', but these would explicitly *not* be the subject of 'academic study'; the college 'could not do everything'. One far-sighted member strengthened this point: rewriting one of the committee's statements of aim ('enabling the students to teach all the ordinary subjects of the . . . curriculum') so as to read, 'producing teachers who can deal effectively in school with the essential elements of a child's education', she added: 'I wish to dissociate myself from any recommendation that instruction be given to any intending teacher in the method of teaching all the subjects of the school curriculum.'

When new curricular policies became effective in the colleges, under A.T.O. supervision, round about 1950, the essential changes were those put forward in these proposals by the committee of 1925. The colleges after the war were faced with the task of providing teachers in substantial numbers for 'the new secondary schools' and continuing to take their traditional part in the development of teaching methods and classroom skills in the, as it were, liberated 'primary schools'. The schools themselves were facing tremendous problems in achieving parity of standards, not only between the new secondary schools, with their many particular problems, and others, but also between the reoriented primary and secondary sectors. 'Parity' is a word that now has muddy edges (and almost no one saw the *curricular* implications of parity, for example in early post-war discussion of projected multilateral secondary schools); but what was at issue was the alleviation of a weight of educational handicap bearing on large sections of the population. And for the first time a common Burnham salary scale set out to emphasize equality of esteem, and perhaps to facilitate transfer of persons, between primary and secondary schools, and among the different kinds of secondary school.

    Enthusiasm for new opportunities laid great stress on the liberalization of attitudes, the setting free of children from 'lockstep' methods of class instruction, the adoption of project and discovery methods of organizing children's learning. This form of enthusiasm was particularly marked in the new primary sector. Something like a distinctive ideology concerning 'the education of young children' was noticeable. A stereotype of a 'college tutor' concerned above all with the freedom and creativity of young children emerged, and seemed worlds removed from those other tutors who prepared for their grammar or public school role those graduates who elected to train for teaching in a university department.

Given the ideological gulf often separating those concerned with 'the young child' from the others, it seems strange that the principle of uniform main courses, identical in content for all student teachers, irrespective of the age of the children they intended to teach, should never have been questioned. The reasons were twofold, two reasons supporting each other. On the one hand the 'main course' was ostensibly for the personal benefit of the student, without necessary connection with her professional intentions. On the other hand, there was a profound indifference to *curriculum* in the educational theory current in the late forties and fifties. Attitudes, personal relationships, ambiance, yes, these were all important (and of course they are); but prior specification of the subject-matter, especially in terms of 'traditional subjects': that was a different and more suspicious matter. Any notion that 'main courses' should be quarries from which to wrest subject matter for infant school lessons would have been most distasteful on educational grounds as encroaching on the rights of the child. Meanwhile the fact of infant students taking exactly the same academic courses as the junior and secondary students—and to the same standards—was a happy symbol and justification of their equal status as educated professionals.

Whatever concern was expressed in the early post-war years on curriculum tended, indeed, to arise from this negative approach to 'subjects'. The word 'subject' was one to be avoided, replaced wherever possible by a term that would stress lack of structure and the freedom to gather together all that was thought relevant on the day—'areas', 'topics', 'fields'. On this the hopes expressed in much of the writing on teaching in the new secondary schools (celebrating their freedom from examination pressures) and the approach common in the primary sector coalesced, and led to experiments in some of the colleges in 'the breaking of subject barriers'. At one college in the late forties, for instance, students were allowed to take two 'grouped courses'—e.g. art and craft, and social studies and general science—and had to take at least

G

one; and the principal explained the point of the distinction
between 'grouped' and 'subject' courses like this: 'It is through
the perception of the relatedness of knowledge that we build up
our conception of truth. . . . The difficulty about our traditional
subject divisions is that they isolate the field of study in a quite
arbitrary fashion . . .', and again, 'The *grouped course* is a starting
point, not a defined end. . . . Its boundaries are intentionally
elastic, and its method stimulates enquiry. . . . The grouped
course must be regarded as a common search . . .'.[4]

Such an approach was sufficiently in line with contemporary
experiments, both in secondary education (the non-selective
schools) and in the primary field, to carry conviction among
some people for some time. Yet most college subject lecturers
would have hesitated to approve this principal's disdainful tone
towards subject disciplines: 'in the old forms of subject work the
lecturer mapped out the route and drove his students along it,
carefully closing all the side gates'. The secondary modern
schools came in time to see their freedom from external examinations as a source of weakness, a self-inflicted disqualification of their
pupils from educational opportunity. Greater knowledge and
sharpened awareness of the importance of sociological determinants of education, after the end of the forties, increasingly
disturbed the preoccupation with education as an 'individual'
concern that had dominated the thirties.[5] And finally the reports
on Piaget's work on cognitive development (which had been
around for some time, but ignored) came to be read, and to raise
questions, not indeed about 'traditional subjects' as such, but
about the developing structure of knowledge; so that it came to
be meaningful to refer to geometry in the infant school, and to
ask what the free activity going on there was for, without one's
being thought a black reactionary.

The subsequent development of opinion and the way it influenced
the perceived role of the 'main courses' in the colleges of education,
can now be sketched as follows.

From about 1950, under new regulations made by the new
Area Training Organizations, each student was required to drop
the clutch of academic courses, five or six in number, which had
comprised the greatest part of his certificate programme, and
concentrate on *one* to be taken 'to as high a pitch as can be
attained'. (The one might extend to two, or to one 'main' with

another 'subsidiary' etc., according to the area.) The aims were still those of 1925: to clear a space for better professional courses and for achievement in one academic field that would set a standard for the individual. Nominally this 'main course' or 'field of study' was not now a straight school teaching-subject, but usually it did broadly correspond to standard school subjects, geography, mathematics, French, biology, and so forth, or to some grouping of them on either a Keele model or a 'study of our civilization' model. The standards aimed at were high, and the work of the best students increasingly came to be recognized as approaching general degree standard; the poorest would be far below. Tutors teaching these main courses were increasingly graduates with good academic teaching experience. They were also fully involved in college teaching practice supervision, and often in providing method courses, and had the opportunity of familiarizing themselves with the various types of school in which their students practised. They could therefore perhaps do something to link the higher level academic work in 'mains' with the logical and psychological issues that arise in devising courses and teaching them in the primary or secondary classroom; questions not only of 'method', but also of the nature and structure of the subject and its place in education, its place in the development of the individual,[6] questions of selection of content, and so forth. The difficulties of finding the right staff, and *for* the staff, at this time are obvious enough; but the opportunities were real; and it is difficult to see what other policy would have served as well at that date.[7]

Further diversification in the range and type of main courses was to take place along lines influenced by changes in the schools and concomitant developments in educational theory.

The study of education can be visualized as specialized along three dimensions: 'developmental', 'disciplinary', and 'curriculum'. By 'developmental' specialization I mean the very necessary separation out of those who know a lot about the young child and his world, and about nursery and infant schools; or about adolescence, or the middle years, and so on, and the schools and curricular arrangements appropriate for them. This is the standard specialization by 'age-range' (or 'phase') in the study of education and growth. This dimension was well established by 1950; and as we have seen it had no particular direct influence on the shape of the new 'main courses'. Its lesson for the teacher, at that date, was characteristically, 'Study the individual and set him free'.

The second dimension of specialization can be called 'disciplinary' for want of a better word. It springs from the recognition that education problems are always in part resolvable into elements susceptible to handling in terms of a variety of autonomous disciplines, which include social, historical and philosophical studies as importantly as psychological. The initials PPHS are now a commonplace for education students. Rather ineffective and unempirical teaching of psychology was in fact common before the forties (it was deplored by an intelligent student training at Cambridge in the 1880s), but the deficiencies of an individualizing psychology as *the* basic educational discipline came to be more obvious in the fifties and sixties, at the same time as more rigorous standards in psychology itself came to be demanded. Sociological studies came to make a greater impact in colleges as they did in the field of national policy-making; studies in language and communication raised new questions about individual cognitive development in the social context— how far, for instance, a child's ability to profit from the free teaching methods used by a Susan Isaacs might depend on family oral background—and the resulting questions were later seen to raise issues that belonged for instance to philosophy of knowledge.

This second major development had an immediate effect both on education departments and on 'main courses'. On education departments the impact was dramatic and, perhaps, exaggerated. The traditional education tutor (this tradition had lasted two decades) who took her students herself through all the aspects of an age-range education course—all aspects of (say, infant school) curriculum and basic skills as well as child development and psychology of learning, teaching methods, school organization, teacher roles and aims of education, the lot—was dismissed as 'mother hen' and replaced by prestigious diploma'd or degreed sociologists and psychologists; or, if not replaced, at least felt herself overshadowed and threatened by them. Acceptance in principle of this line of change was well on the way in education departments by 1966. Meanwhile the range of 'main courses' on offer was also affected in two ways. The characteristic lesson for the teacher was now clearly no longer, 'Study the individual'; it was, 'Understand the social context, study your pupils in relation to their family and environment, clarify your own social role and aims'. Hence 'main courses' now offered either in education, aiming to provide students with the opportunity of more advanced work in the 'disciplines'; or in the disciplines themselves—in psychology, philosophy, sociology—and in addition the 'main courses' which followed on the recommendations of the Newsom Report,[8] in social work, and the like.

Meanwhile, rising standards in student intake and in the academic status of the colleges led to greater self-confidence in devising mainstream 'subject' courses; and in this development the changing climate of opinion after the foundation of Keele and other post-war universities helped. Grouped courses were now more carefully thought out and recognized the need for 'structure'; the Keele foundation year, the Sussex non-departmental structure, came to be influences.

Outlining for instance in 1967 a course of college training designed to equip students for teaching the 'Newsom secondary child', Raynor commented on part of the scheme entitled 'Modern Studies', to which history, sociology, geography and science departments all contributed, that their hope 'in using these inter-disciplinary approaches' was

> not to pursue the myth of integrated knowledge, but rather to indicate to students how they may employ this method in schools, once they themselves are familiar with the concepts which lie within the different frameworks of knowledge

and adds crucially, with a glance back at the late forties,

> One of the real difficulties here is to explore with students fresh approaches to the traditional curriculum while safeguarding them from making the errors used twenty years ago. . . . Far better to revise the methods used within the traditional subjects structure where the concepts are known than to have a topic approach when one is not clear about the concepts that have to be taught.[9]

Now, this was not itself a 'main course'; but nor was it a standard 'education department' course or 'curriculum' course. Aiming to meet a precise need, it included elements of all three: a 'subsidiary main' course in sociology or psychology for each student ('we do not believe that the courses provided in either the sociology of education or in educational psychology are in themselves sufficient. . . . The problem of exploring with the students the wide range of social and industrial roles that pupils will have to be initiated into calls for more time'); curriculum courses and professional courses covering a variety of fields; and links in addition with any standard 'main course'. Not only, it is plain, has the somewhat vague approach to integrated courses noticed at the beginning of our period been replaced by an intellectually tougher and adventurous grasp at the possibilities of 'inter- disciplinary approaches', but the college course itself has become interdisciplinary; and thus is completed the third revolution by which the 'main courses' themselves, without ceasing to be educative, become professional in a large number of explicit ways. A rationale has been found for the third dimension, that of 'curriculum', in education studies.

This is where we are at. Not two dimensions, but three, are involved in the study of education; and it is odd that for so long anyone should have conceived of education studies as specialized along the dimensions of, first the sequential development of children; and then of the four now conventional 'disciplines' (PPHS); yet overlooked what 'schooling' means to ordinary folk—the content of instruction and learning, the intellectual skills and conceptualizations which make up the texture and fabric of the growing and educated mind. Because, when all is said and done, the unifying area, the starting point and touch- stone, must be curriculum.[10] It would make a fascinating subject in intellectual history (or the sociology of knowledge) to trace the rise and decline of that indifference to content, that rejection of the notion of preconceived subject-matter, curriculum, which lies (but only just) in the immediate past, and made this omission even conceivable.[11]

At this point we have to begin to peer into the future. It will have become clear why a new *rationale* for the college of education 'main course' as an element in teacher education is now needed; and why at the same time one has had to be patient about this. There are right and wrong moments for crystallization. Voices have continuously pressed for the college of education course to be structured around the study of 'education' as understood at a particular time. Had this been acted on in the heyday of the differential psychologists—with their apparent support for streaming, for the 11+, for the tripartite secondary system—or at the time of the first enthusiasm for sociology, with its great emphasis on social class—the colleges would now be in a less strong position to offer a course of training capable of linking curricular knowledge coherently with the other disciplines mentioned.

No one will imagine that curriculum theory is itself yet in a very finished or advanced state, or that linking the fast developing knowledge in this field to 'developmental' studies and the other educational considerations that influence it and are influenced by it will be easy. Vast national curriculum development projects have grown up (partly for accidental reasons) without any but minimal or purely personal links with the colleges offering initial training; and they have themselves engaged in single-subject programmes rather than whole-curriculum studies. No whole-curriculum study of such a sector of higher education as (say) teacher education has, so far as I know, been attempted. But the area is being investigated more rapidly and more systematically than ever in the recent past, and the results will be important for the colleges of education. One consequence will be to bring main-course tutors and departments more fully and coherently into joint programmes with those whose special fields are child and human development, and so on, in a genuinely interdisciplinary study of education itself at that point where the development of new syllabuses and teaching methods in schools, the in-service programmes, and initial training can fruitfully interact.

Thus by maintaining and strengthening their academic departments—by doing so not least, thanks to the wisdom of the 1957 Ministry proposals, at the time of the extension of the training course to three years[12]—the colleges have safeguarded the possibility of putting the study of *curriculum* right in the centre, where it belongs, and of recognizing the 'main course' as the main vehicle for each student's understanding in depth of what curriculum is about. In this context the Balance of Training policy of the sixties, whereby four out of every five college students were directed away from the secondary to the primary field, may have had its good side. The main courses had to be seen as 'good enough for primary teachers'.

Good enough, may be; but how relevant? We have seen how

main courses in educational 'disciplines', as well as in other branches of knowledge of instrumental value for teachers in any sector (like social work) have extended the traditional list. We have noticed conspectus courses now more sharply defined and rigorous than some of the early prototypes. But what about the standard school subjects—geography, history, mathematics, English—taken at 'main course' level? What about French, geology, Russian?

Here it would be unrealistic to ignore the extent to which the syllabus, the teaching methods, and the general grip and approach exemplified in the work of the *subject* departments in the colleges have influenced, as well as been influenced by, what is happening in schools and above all in the education of children between the age of school entry and the end of the middle-school years (about thirteen). For long it has not been just a question of tacking a few thoughts on 'methodology' onto purely academic courses of university type, still less of providing courses based on existing school syllabuses; but of providing future teachers with the concepts, the knowledge of facts, structures and principles, to enable them to recast and reconstruct a syllabus in, say, mathematics. Mathematics illustrates the point well; college of education staff have played a part (e.g. through the education section of the A.T.C.D.E.) with others in a very thorough reform of primary and secondary syllabuses, and as a result college of education 'main courses' now have a vital transitional role in enabling many adult students to understand junior work! But what is true for mathematics is true, in greater or lesser degrees, or should be, for scientific, linguistic, environmental, musical, religious, . . . knowledge. The language of the 1925 report is out of date, but the key point was understood then: what our teachers need from their training course is not more and more facts, but it *is* a grasp of the principles underlying the subjects of instruction. The explosion of publicly available knowledge has combined with new policies on staff work in primary schools to create a new context for the college of education 'main course'.[13]

It is arguable therefore that the college 'main course' in, say, mathematics is now the most valuable source for the 'semi-specialists', as some would call them, offering, and able, to take responsibility for mathematical guidance of their colleagues on the staff of an infant or junior school; while the corresponding 'curriculum' (non-main) course will be looking after more modestly equipped 'followers' or supporters (in mathematics). Most notably, these 'main courses' may play a key part in enabling the critical sector of the middle school to evade the disastrous choice between bad stereotypes of both secondary and primary—either a bleak examination grind or sloppy activity methods—by enabling schools to develop and find staff capable of the tough-minded radicalism mentioned above as notable in a 'Newsom secondary course'. Once this possibility is envisaged, the 'main courses' have to be perceived as relevant to the professional destination as well as the personal development of the student in ways extending far beyond 'methodology'; and that is why it is now beside the point to ask, what is the relevance of 'main course' French, or geology, to a future infant teacher? The main course is more than a quarry of lesson material (with 'method' possibly tacked on), and perfectly intelligible answers to such a question can be given. Once the *professional* relevance of the 'main course' has been explicitly recognized, outside as well as within the colleges, a greater coherence of approach and collaborative deployment of staff in training, teaching, and in the study of education, will be possible.

The actual administrative arrangements and regulations should not be sacrosanct. One wonders, for instance, whether the inflexible restriction of each student to one 'main course' (where this applies) is necessary; or whether, under guidance in the light of individual background and preference, a student might not be allowed to experiment with a wider range. None of the arguments against such flexibility has struck me as wholly conclusive.[14] The direction of change seems likely to bring about greater diversity and specialization among the different colleges, and such a continuation of the gradual tendency throughout this century would be no bad thing. The present diversity of 'main course' options from college to college has opened up fields that could not have been envisaged in any uniform national list; conversely, a subject like housecraft, formerly available in many general colleges, is now confined (as a frankly professional 'main course'!) to a small number of colleges where it can be strong. If strength could be reinforced in the case of some other certificate and especially B.Ed. main courses, there might be more than economic benefits.

In general the relationship between 'main courses' and 'curriculum courses' needs thorough review. One sad side-effect of the post-McNair 'main course' was to leave curriculum studies in an administrative limbo, to be taught often at the discretion of the college and sometimes of the individual tutor, examined if at all by the pragmatic test of their effect as contributions to efficient teaching on school practice. (It is sufficiently clear by now that the difficulty of assessing teaching ability is great enough without this extraneous complication.) What the right solutions are is still far from clear. It is more than ever true that 'instruction in the method of teaching all the subjects of the school curriculum' cannot and should not be given to anybody. There are implications for schools there—for staffs and managers. What is also true and concerns the colleges directly is that the links between main courses and curriculum courses will have to be taught. It is no good hoping that they will be noticed; they have to be taught. The Newsom course from the description of which I quoted earlier is valuable for exemplifying this point.

But, if taught, they ought perhaps to be examined—though not necessarily by any particular type of formal examination. That would seem to be the thinking underlying a movement, now visible simultaneously in different parts of the country, to bring together all the ancillary 'curriculum courses' and 'professional courses' and subsume them under one global title—to be examined as in effect one course at 'main course' level. On the analogy of the Third World, this notion has been called 'third area'—as good a generic shorthand title for it as any; as it carries the assumption that in the examination of certificate studies equal weight will go to three areas: a 'main course', the 'third area', and theory of education.

Certificate studies, or B.Ed. studies—the advent of the B.Ed. degree has probably had a less disruptive effect on the college of education curriculum than was expected. (Its positive effects are not my concern here.) In spite of exceptions and pockets of intransigence, the risk of which is inherent in so decentralized an authoritarian system as the universities (to coin a new synonym for academic freedom), certificate-type subject courses seem on the whole to have been accepted into the university degree system with their professional direction and integrity surprisingly intact. (A slow trend to move towards a 'three years plus one year' course structure, under which the whole certificate course may count in effect as Part I for the degree, may be helpful.) Broadly, the recognition of college-based studies for university degrees has opened up the avenue of further academic study for many college students and given a deserved injection of self-confidence to all, without serious deformation of the traditional courses. Above all it has not meant that the B.Ed. 'main courses' became so 'academic' and so different as to be appropriate for secondary specialist teaching but no longer right for the primary phase. An association between a B.Ed. degree and the following of a course inappropriate for a primary teacher was of course to be avoided. Hence now the importance of securing that proposals of the 'third area' type, which mean examining at 'main course' level composite programmes of curriculum and professional studies, should be acceptable at B.Ed. level; and that in the course of their passage through B.Ed. syllabus committees they should not cease to be appropriate to the preparation of infant, junior, and middle-school teachers. There is serious danger in construing 'relevance' too narrowly, and overlooking the educative and not merely professional functions of the whole college course. There is also danger if relevance is overlooked entirely.

At this point the track peters out in the uncertainties of the future. I believe the colleges have been right in holding on to their 'main courses', and that it is now necessary to find a more convincing and sharply argued rationale for these than has been current over the last twenty years. I have tried to sketch the basis of such a rationale in the course of surveying the way main courses have been developed in the two decades of their existence, and to make some suggestions for the future.

One additional point may be made. Some three-quarters of the teachers now in posts in colleges of education are 'main course' specialists, appointed for their competence in a subject field (among other things). Their job has usually meant their being fully committed, not always in ideal conditions from anyone's point of view, in exploring with students professional and vocational aspects of their subject, and co-operating with education tutors in curriculum and method courses and the like. If the concurrent course as it is here presented has no solid rationale to support it, it is right that they should be redeployed in teaching polytechnic, university, or liberal arts courses in their subjects, or return to primary and secondary school teaching. They could contribute valuably to academic teaching in non-vocational courses; Tibble has made the point pungently that, for instance, most undergraduate courses are insufficiently educative.[15] But if the argument of these pages is well founded, the fund of knowledge and experience represented by these teachers is a large and unusual resource at the disposal of the education service. In that case its availability in and through the college of education of the future, as an important crossing and meeting point for career teachers, can be reckoned as sheer bonus.

Notes and References

1 Alternative names: 'main subject', 'main field of study', 'principal subject', 'special subject'. For the present purpose 'these terms can be taken as synonymous'.
2 On this, see the editor's introduction to Wiseman, S., ed. (1961), *Examinations and English Education*, Manchester University Press; and Oakeshott, M., 'Education: the engagement and its frustration', in *Proceedings of the Philosophy of Education Society of Great Britain*, V, 1, Oxford, 1970.
3 Board of Education (1925), *Report of the Departmental Committee on the Training of Teachers for Public Elementary Schools*, Cmd. 2409.
4 Jordan, D. (1949), 'A student prepares', *Bulletin of Education*, 18–19.
5 Nunn, T. P., *Education: Its First Data and Principles*, which appeared in many editions and was a formative influence on graduates who trained in the late twenties and thirties.
6 When I was head of a languages department in a college of education I took the view that the production of specialist teachers was one, but only one, task for the department; and that this like other 'subject' departments had its own particular incidental contributions to make to an understanding of education—for instance, in the comparative field, and in relation to the place of language in child development. A convincing case that subject specialists have a special contribution to make to developmental studies was made in Professor Peters' address to an A.T.C.D.E. Education Section/D.E.S. conference, on 'Education as a specific preparation for teaching' (*The Education and Training of Teachers: Professional Concern or Academic Discipline?*, D.E.S., 1967.) See also chapter 1 in Peters, R. S., ed. (1969), *Perspectives on Plowden*, Routledge & Kegan Paul. Solid fundamental work on development in relation to curriculum still remains a major need.
7 Lecturers in the older training colleges had often, according to the testimony of the 1925 Report, passed from school to college as students and stayed on as lecturers without intervening teaching experience in any school.
8 Central Advisory Council for Education (England) (1963) *Half our Future*, H.M.S.O.

9 Raynor, J. M. (1967), 'Training teachers for the Newsom child', *Education for Teaching*, No. 73.

10 See for instance Kerr, J. F. (1968), ed., *Changing the Curriculum*, University of London Press; and note the appearance of the new *Journal for Curriculum Studies*, the widespread discussion of working papers from 'the Schools Council for the Curriculum and Examinations' (formed in the mid-sixties from an examinations council); the establishment of the Goldsmiths College Curriculum Laboratory.

11 A deservedly influential volume, Tibble, J. W. (1966), ed., *The Study of Education*, Routledge & Kegan Paul, which marked and consolidated the shift from a 'developmental' to a 'disciplinary' approach to its subject, contains in 250 pages no more than two or three paragraphs on the curriculum.

12 Ministry of Education (1957), *The Training of Teachers: Suggestions for a Three-year Training College Course*, H.M.S.O., Pamphlet No. 34.

13 The Committee of 1925 already referred to (Note 3, above), when it looked at 'the tendency of future organization', thought that in the bigger (elementary) schools there could be 'some measure of specialization of teaching'; each teacher might teach 'one or two subjects throughout the school'.

14 The regulations for the University of London Teacher's Certificate have for some years given an opportunity to students to take a second (and in theory a third) main course, including main courses either in a *discipline* ('a specialized aspect of the theory and practice of education') or *curriculum and teaching method* ('the content and methods of teaching a selected subject of the curriculum'). In practice most students have been taking one main course, and on this matter none more than two; and the liberty of choice seems to have been exercised by colleges rather than individual candidates.

15 Tibble J. W. (1966), ed., *The Study of Education, op. cit.*, pp. 232-3.

Many students and ex-students, when asked to evaluate their course in a college or department of education, say that the most valuable part of it was the periods of practice in the schools. At the same time one of the commonest criticisms of the college and department courses made by experienced teachers is that there is not enough emphasis on the learning of practical skills and too much on 'theory'. Students too are liable to complain that they do not receive enough help with difficulties such as class control, how to deal with difficult children or help backward readers or slow learners in general.

Now I think we must begin by recognizing that this is an area of learning where we must especially expect unrealistic mixed with realistic criticisms from the learner or ex-learner. For most people, learning to function as a reasonably competent, confident and equable teacher is a longish, complex and at times painful process in which feelings of inadequacy, humiliation and personal affront are liable to occur. A student, because of the school he is in, the relatively short periods of practice and the help he is getting from staff, may not in fact experience those feelings at that stage. All that this means is that he has not yet been tested on some fundamental points. Unless he is very exceptional, or very lucky, he will face these tests early in his career after appointment. Whenever he meets them it is natural for him to feel that his tutors at college should have taught him how to avoid or cope with the particular difficulties he is experiencing. He tends to assume that this could have been done by some kind of 'telling' or teaching, by hints and tips of the 'how to' 'how not to' kind. One has to say categorically that there are no short cuts to learning how to become an effective teacher in the normal range of circumstances. A minority of students appear to have the necessary skills already or to pick them up quickly and easily; for most, longer time, considerable experience and varying degrees of failure and tribulation have to be undergone. This does not, however, mean that no help can be given, that the best we can do is push the learner in at the deep end and hope he will manage to swim. On the contrary, it is my belief that a very special kind of help is needed but that the current method of organizing and supervising block practices makes it very difficult for the right kind of help to be given. How has it come about that for a good many years now we have been operating a system of supervision that is, as all agree, expensive in terms of money, time and energy, but also, I suggest, relatively ineffective in terms of giving students the kind of help they need?

The answer to this question is to be found in the historic development of teacher education over the past 100 years or so. What we had to begin with, in the middle nineteenth century, was a system of apprenticeship training. Pupil-teachers were attached to master-teachers and continued their own education while gradually picking up, by imitation and practice, the skills involved in organizing and giving lessons to groups of children, often quite large groups who learned 'simultaneously'. The early training colleges took over this apprenticeship training from the schools and adapted it. The professional training in class and school management and methods of teaching was the province of a Master (or Mistress) of Method. He was usually in charge of a school, called a 'demonstration' or 'practice' school, attached to the college: and the practical training of the students took place largely in that school. The students observed model lessons and gave 'criticism' lessons in the presence of staff and other students. It was still in essence an apprenticeship system with the Master of Method and other teachers in the practice school as the mastercraftsmen. And this system persisted in essence well into the twentieth century.

In the period after the first world war however changes occurred which made anachronisms of both pupil-teachers and masters of method: and with their passing, I suggest, the fundamental apprenticeship link was broken: but we have continued to operate *as if it were still there*, i.e. as if the benefits of it were still there though the circumstances are quite different. With the expansion of training after 1902, colleges became larger and the demonstration or practice school no longer sufficed for the practical work; many more schools had to be used and these had no special links with the college. At the same time, changes in aims and techniques, particularly in primary education, made the whole idea of formal lessons and standardized methods for doing this and that seem outmoded; the term master of method gradually disappeared and was replaced by lecturer in education. These changes were not, however, accompanied by a fundamental re-thinking about how best to help students to acquire the necessary skills in these changed conditions. Each lecturer in education, and as numbers grew, many lecturers in other subjects, had a group of about twelve 'apprentice' students attached to him in school practice periods. But he is no longer the master-craftsman alongside whom they work sharing the daily traffic of the classroom, observing each other, dealing with the same children. He is able to visit his students about twice a week, a good half of his time being spent in travel from school to school (or in other college duties). The person the student *is* in daily contact with in an apprenticeship situation is the class or subject teacher in the school. *But* however much help the student in fact gets from the teacher (and this varies enormously), we have to note that the teacher is not officially responsible for the student: at the best it is a divided responsibility, at the worst the teacher may withhold help for fear of interfering or feel resentment that someone so fleeting and remote as the college tutor should be thought better able to help than the person on the spot and responsible for the children in question.

This is a situation which breeds stereotypes, and sure enough they abound. Despite good (in most cases) personal relationships between school and college staff, one does often feel that the relationship is based, as someone once said of the marriage relationship, 'on a mutual misunderstanding'. It is not uncommon for young teachers, joining a school staff, to hear a comment from someone that now they can forget all the cloudy theorizing they learned at college and get down to brass tacks. This is often linked with the belief that most college lecturers have had no relevant teaching experience. In a recent article in the *Daily Telegraph*, its education correspondent wrote: 'There are no firm statistics to show exactly how many college lecturers have taught at schools. But it is widely accepted that only a few have taught.'[1] He might, indeed he ought, to have consulted Professor W. Taylor's *Society and the Education of Teachers* which reports the results of a survey on this very question. 'Overall, about one in eleven of the men and one in twelve of the women had no experience in the classroom, a third of the men and a quarter of the women had between one and six years' teaching experience, 53 per cent of both sexes had between seven and eighteen years and 5 per cent of the men and 10 per cent of the women had taught for more than nineteen years.'[2] Of lecturers responsible for professional courses in education, only 4 per cent (presumably specialists in sociology, psychology, etc.) were without school experience. It is also worth noting that the tutors in question, in addition to their own teaching experience, visit many different schools in the course of their supervising of students and have a much wider knowledge of what is going on in schools than the teacher whose experience has perforce been limited to one or two schools.

What is wrong then in the present situation does not arise from the lack of practical experience of the supervising tutor or in his failure to value practical experience highly. What is wrong is that the system within which he has to operate does not provide the conditions necessary for giving the students the most effective support and assistance in the acquiring of practical skills. This is not only because two visits a week in the role mostly of a non-participant observer of what is going on in the classroom are a quite inadequate basis for an *apprenticeship* relationship. It is also because the tutor has another role, in fact, of which the student cannot but be aware; it is that of an assessor or inspector. Now it is notoriously difficult, for psychological reasons, to operate simultaneously the assessing role and the helping role— they tend to contradict each other. Tutors when taxed with this reply by playing down the assessing role, saying they only do this at the end of a practice, or perhaps that their relationship with the student is so good that the assessing does not get in the way of the helping. This may be so in the case of a competent student who knows she is good; it can hardly be so for the majority of students.[3]

The irony in all this is that no one has ever proved that assessment in the form of attaching a five to thirteen point teaching grade to each student is necessary or useful. It was in fact taken over as a tradition by the Joint Examinations Boards in the 1920s along with other Board of Education procedures for the award of a national certificate. The post-McNair institutes took it over in turn, again without any re-examination of its validity: a number of institutes have simplified the grading in recent years and advocacy for a pass-fail grading has grown in strength. But most continue to grade on a five-point scale at least and have elaborate procedures for visits by assessors from other colleges and by external examiners to check grading. A Manchester survey comparing school practice gradings with head teachers' assessments

H

after five years showed low correlation—as one would expect
from consideration of the number of variables involved at any
particular assessment point.[4] Should we continue to use instruments which imply much more precise measurement than can
possibly be achieved?

For whose benefit, then, are these assessments made? It can
hardly be for the benefit of the student, for in most universities
the marks may not be divulged—one or two pioneers have
recently altered this rule in the case of school practice marks.
The student knows he is being assessed but does not know
the outcome (or knows it only in general terms, not as a precise
mark). And the price paid for this is the role conflict referred
to above whereby the tutor's helping function is diminished and
contradicted in varying degrees by the inspecting and assessing
function.

It is difficult not to caricature this system: a factual description
of it would read like a caricature. I recommend, for example, a
survey by a college or A.T.O. in which time spent in discussion
with students is the numerator and time spent getting there plus
time spent sitting in observing is the denominator. Then cost
the operations. One suspects that what we are dealing with here
is in a similar category to the shadow gesture of defiance which
the rat at the feeding trough gives on the appearance of another
rat (there being enough food and to spare): so do we preserve, at
great expense, a vestigial reference to an apprenticeship system,
which, as far as tutor and student are concerned in a block practice
context, is long defunct?

I turn now to consider what changes can be made in the
arrangements for school practice to avoid or remedy the disadvantages referred to above. In recent years a number of innovations and experiments have been undertaken in colleges and
departments which provide basis for speculation about future
developments on a larger scale. Some of these are concerned
with variations in the arrangements for block practice; others
are concerned with forms of practice other than the block
practice.

The defects I have referred to are not criticisms of the concept
of the block practice itself, i.e. the attachment of the student to
a school for a continuous period ranging from several weeks to a
full term. The full-term practice (or in some cases two half terms
with a period of study between) is usual today in most department

courses training graduates. In the college three-year courses, there has been a marked tendency of late to lengthen the period of the final practice to nine weeks or more. This is because the advantages to the student (and the school in most cases) of having as long a period as possible under conditions approximating as closely as may be to those of full-time employment are well recognized. The student has longer to find his feet, to get to know children and staff, to gain confidence, to make mistakes and have time to correct them. The longer period in one school becomes a disadvantage only in the case of a minority of students who for some reason make a really bad start or run into serious problems in the early days. It is usually difficult if not impossible for them to remedy the situation in the context in which the problems occurred whereas often, though not always, they can do so given a new setting and a fresh start. Fitting students to schools, and changing them when necessary, is a skill school practice organizers become adept at. Some schools (and classes and teachers within schools) do well by average to good students but are not good with a student who has fundamental problems in adapting to being a teacher. Other schools also excel in helping problem students and enabling them to find a way out of their difficulties and become useful teachers.

This leads me to the observation that the value of the block practice derives fundamentally from its being the modern form of the apprenticeship relationship which was embodied in the pupil-teacher system and in the practice schools of the early colleges. It is indeed the only sound basis for the acquisition of practical skills. These can only be acquired by the student's attempting to do the job in a work situation; and in so far as he will benefit from help and guidance, this is best given by a more experienced person whose work this is. The prevailing system of supervision recognizes this up to a point; all tutors are aware of and grateful for the help given to students by the teachers they are working with (and equally aware of the lamentable consequences when this help is not forthcoming or not effective). But the prevailing system then proceeds to distort and diminish the value of the apprenticeship principle by officially making the apprentice master not the school teacher in day to day relationship with the student, but the college tutor who in this context has only occasional and tenuous contacts with the work situation in this school, who is, as one teacher put it, only a 'passing cloud' as far as the school is concerned. What we need, I suggest, is a fuller recognition, making more of a reality of the apprenticeship relationship between student and school.

Recognition of this has led in recent years to a number of experiments in the appointment by departments and colleges of school-based tutors or teacher tutors who are given fuller responsibility for the day to day supervision of a student's (or in some cases a group of students') work. Leicester University School of Education, for example, has operated a system of teacher-tutors in varying forms over the past ten years and it has grown from small beginnings to well over 100 appointments today. The teacher-tutors work closely with members of the school staff, are consulted on relevant matters and receive honoraria for their services. Several other university departments have similar schemes. Some colleges also (e.g. Bede College, Durham) have experimented with teacher-tutors. The time is ripe for a much wider application of this practice. The Universities Council for the Education of Teachers is currently discussing the various forms of operation and types of responsibility and is discussing the problems involved with the other professional associations. Most of these, in their statements to the Select Committee on Teacher Education and elsewhere have expressed strong support for the principle and indeed for many years have urged that the schools be given fuller responsibilities in this field. The grounds for co-operation exist. What would be helpful in the present situation would be discussions at the national level of the administrative and financial implications, e.g. whether teachers accepting fuller responsibilities should be paid for this work and if so, whether by responsibility allowances or by *ad hoc* payments for extra work done outside normal hours of work.

The question that arises for the colleges and departments is how would such a development for fuller school responsibility affect the role and work of the tutors. Objections often made from this angle to the developments in question stress that (a) the students, as such,[5] must remain the overall responsibility of the college or department, and (b) it would be undesirable to cut off the lecturers so responsible from their present contacts with schools and practical work.

I hasten to add that no system of supervision which I am advocating should have these consequences. The college's and tutor's overall responsibility remains: what changes is the way it is exercised. He delegates some things in order to do other things better. He works through and with the teacher-tutor rather than directly with the student. He visits the schools for this purpose, obviously not as frequently as at present, so valuable time will be saved. He invites his group of teacher-tutors to the college occasionally for discussion of common problems. If he visits a student in class it should be, I suggest, on invitation rather than by right, except where a question of the student's fitness to continue has arisen. It is also important, in my view, that the selection and appointment of teacher-tutors is a college responsibility, subject to the approval of head teachers and L.E.A.s. Not all teachers want this kind of responsibility; not all are as good at helping students as they may be with children, and not all, let it be said, are good with children. Some schools have special difficulties which may make them unsuitable for this purpose. I envisage that for some years to come at any rate we should have to operate a mixed system in which the extra responsibility is delegated in some cases but not in others.[6]

Assuming the use of teacher-tutors, there is however an alternative form of supervision which the college tutor can use with a student or group of students which is not based on direct observation of practical work by the tutor. It is, in fact, based on the tutor's *not* having been present for the lesson period to be discussed. He asks instead for a detailed account by the student of what happened and uses this to help the student to make a self-assessment. An experiment in the use of this 'protocol' method, which derives from G. Caplan's work in social-work training, was carried out at Leicester some years ago and has been regularly used since by members of staff at St Gabriel's College.[7]

This method would seem to have a number of advantages:
1. It reduces considerably the conflict mentioned above between the tutor's helping and judging roles.
2. The student is encouraged and trained in habits of observation, recall and recording.
3. The student is more deeply involved in the evaluation process. The tutor relies on him to produce the material for evaluation, and he does not feel as is likely in the other situation, 'That is your business. That is what you are here for. Why should I do it for you?'

4. Suggestions for alternative procedures or improvements in technique are more likely to be effective when occurring in this setting, produced either by the student himself or as a result of a co-operative process and not as external criticism.[8]

It should be added that the effective use of this form of super-vision requires (a) that the tutor has had considerable experience in the classroom at the level being dealt with, i.e. it could not be used by a tutor whose own experience had been in the secondary field for supervision of infants' teachers, and (b) that the tutor has had some training in the use of this kind of supervision. The tutor needs to be aware, for example, of the extent to which the student, in discussing his problems with children, is being affected by his own problems with regard to people in authority including the tutor. The latter will not, as in a therapeutic relation-ship, aim at making the student overtly aware of this: but his own assessment of it will underlie his questions and comments about the happenings in the classroom. This kind of discussion, whether with individual students or in a group setting, can also be a most suitable occasion for the close relating of theory to practice, which is a contribution the college tutor can best make. What I am saying is that if they both supervise the same student, the contributions of college tutor and teacher-tutor should be complementary, each doing what he is best fitted to do, and not as often at present duplicative or possibly contradictory.

I turn now to forms of practice other than block periods. In these also there has been some experiment in recent years, though in fact the basis of it existed years ago in some departments and colleges which sent out their students into schools for any-thing from half a day to two days a week, the rest of the week being spent in study. The main point of this concurrent practice (though it was not always utilized in the older forms referred to) is the opportunities it affords (a) for tutors and students (and possibly also teachers in schools) working together on some practical scheme or project, and (b) for then relating theory and practice closely in the subsequent discussion of the work in college. This 'study practice', involving tutors other than education tutors, and providing much of the material for the study of education in that year of the course, was pioneered at St Luke's College some years ago and is now in varying forms a common device. It should be noted that the disadvantages of the inspectorial type of supervision by the college tutor are removed in a different way in this system: it is a genuine apprenticeship relationship between student and tutor because the latter is actively engaged in the practice, not present as a non-participant observer, is exposing himself to observation and criticism along with the students. It is my opinion that this concurrent practice is most valuable in the middle stages of the course when students have acquired some basis both of theoretical study and of practical experience in schools. There is still considerable difference of opinion about how best to acquire the latter in the early part of the course, whether by preliminary short block practices or by another form of concurrent practice, mainly providing for observation and participation with individual children or small groups. There is of course also the problem of providing a variety of experience over the whole course so that the student has some awareness of what is going on at stages earlier and later than the stage of his special interest.

To sum up, what I hope we shall see in the next decade is a widespread adoption of practices which already exist in a great variety of experimental forms. They have this in common: that they all involve the willing assumption of greater responsibility by the schools for the practical education of teachers. This should *relieve* the colleges and departments to have more time for the other responsibilities they have taken on in recent years such as B.Ed. courses, and participation in in-service training and curriculum development schemes. But it does not mean that they opt out of responsibility for practical work: they use the time they have for it in ways which augment and complement the contribution of the schools. In this way the partnership between colleges and schools can become even more fruitful and need not be confined, indeed, to helping the development of students: colleges and departments of education are well equipped to function as regional teacher centres supplementing the local centres now established.

Notes and References

1 'How are the teachers taught?', the *Daily Telegraph*, 6 November 1970.
2 *Op. cit.*, 1969, Faber & Faber, p. 212.

3 For students' attitudes to school practice see Cope, E., *Education for Teaching*, No. 80 (1969), No. 81 (1970).

4 Wiseman, S., and Start, K. B. (1965), *B.J.E.P.*, 35, pp. 342–61. Other surveys have produced conflicting evidence. See *Teaching Practice: A Bibliography*, issued by the Cambridge Institute, for other references.

5 There are, in fact, under discussion variant forms of graduate training which envisage the incorporation of the probationary year in a two-year course. The trainees then, for half the period or more, would be appointees to a school staff and in receipt of a basic salary.

6 Tibble, J. W. (1966). 'Practical work training in the education of teachers', in *Education for Teaching*, No. 70, May 1966.
Baker, J. R. (1967), 'Teacher co-tutor scheme', in *Education for Teaching*, No. 73, Summer.

7 See Caspari, I. E., and Eggleston, S. J. (1965), 'A new approach to supervision of teaching practice', in *Education for Teaching*, No. 68, November.
Clark, J. M. (1967), 'Supervision of teaching practice', in *Education for Teaching*, Autumn.
Caplan, G. (1961), *An Approach to Community Mental Health*, Tavistock.

8 Tibble, J. W. (1969), 'Insight training in the education of teachers', in *Interaction*, ed., Paul de Berker, Cassirer.

Alternative Forms of Training Within the University

The present one-year course of 'training' in the universities was not always for all students limited to one academic year. The university departments of education were established with two purposes in mind: to provide a one-year postgraduate course for secondary-school teachers, i.e. grammar-school teachers; and to provide a four-year degree plus training course for 'elementary' school teachers. The second of these courses took time to develop and grew out of normal two-year certificate courses as the quality of the students improved, until eventually all of them took the degree course. But for many years in some departments certificate students sat side by side with degree students in the same university classes, and all education students preparing for the elementary schools took courses in the principles and practice of teaching, hygiene, physical education, and music or an art or craft subject, as well as in practical teaching, some of which were provided during the undergraduate years.

On the other hand the work of the one-year secondary students was confined to the postgraduate year, since they did not identify themselves as intending teachers until shortly before graduation. As one might expect, the 'secondary' pattern gradually superseded the 'elementary' pattern for a variety of reasons. One was that the regulations allowed students to transfer to the secondary course, thereby relieving themselves of the obligation to qualify in the additional subjects; another was that as the number of State Scholarships and Local Authority Major Awards increased, the 'secondary' students, uncommitted to teaching as undergraduates increased in number, although they did not become the majority in some departments until after the second world war. Another factor was the increase in the number of secondary schools, hastened by Hadow reorganization, so that the aim of providing a substantial intake of graduates into the elementary schools was frustrated, most of them going into the new secondary schools or at any rate into the reorganized senior departments: and the 'secondary' type of training therefore became the appropriate type for the majority of students.

The four-year system was finally extinguished by the Ministry of Education, acting on the advice of the National Advisory

Council for the Training and Supply of Teachers, in 1951, and with it went the possibility of bringing forward any elements of the training course, however insignificant they had become, into the undergraduate years. The only possibility left open was the inclusion of some elements of educational studies in the degree course proper, and this matter is discussed below.

The nature of the postgraduate course can best be realized by describing one such course, even if it is not quite typical. The students are asked after they have been accepted to write a vacation essay on an aspect of education. They arrive in the third week of September and take a rapid one-week 'orientation' course in which the pattern of studies and its possibilities are explained and the approach to teaching is discussed. They then go into schools, most into primary and secondary modern schools, and some into comprehensive schools, for a short period of three weeks of initial teaching practice, during which they are helped by the staff of the schools and visited by their tutors. They return to the department for an eight-week course of lectures, discussions and written work, during which they take part in method courses in their subjects, courses in the principles, history and philosophy of education, and courses in aspects of educational psychology and child development, with some provision also for studies in special subjects among which they may make a choice.

In the second term of the year they return to the schools, mainly to grammar and comprehensive schools, for a further ten-week period of teaching practice, with an emphasis on the teaching of their special subjects. Again they are helped by the staff of the schools and visited by their tutors. They return to the department for tutorial discussions and *ad hoc* courses for a few days, and spend the Easter vacation writing a dissertation, the topic having been agreed with their tutor and investigated during the long teaching practice.

In the third term of the year they return to the department for a further period of eight weeks, the first six weeks being devoted to resumed method courses and lecture courses in educational studies, again including studies in optional special subjects, the final two weeks being devoted to the preparation of work in connection with their method courses. A written examination consisting of two papers in the principles of education is taken at the end of the lecture courses, and the method work is assessed at the end of the course, which finishes in mid-June.

For the remainder of the month of June the students are free, while the staff are occupied with the reading of examination scripts and method work. The dissertations have meanwhile been presented at the beginning of the third term and assessed before the written examination begins.

It is obvious that a course such as this is all too short. It consists of thirteen weeks of practical teaching and seventeen weeks of theoretical studies, with substantial work in the Easter vacation added. The McNair Committee which reported in 1944 bluntly stated that they had considered and rejected the proposal that the postgraduate course should be lengthened to two years but pointed out that there was no reason why it should not run from the beginning of September to the end of July, with vacations of school rather than university length. The examining procedure could be simplified and shortened, but staffing would need to be improved if the longer course were not to make undue inroads into staff vacations.

Since the 'specimen' course briefly described above may not be typical, it is important to add an account of variants which exist, and to show how they differ, before we consider changes within the one-year framework which have been advocated.

First, teaching practice needs to be considered. Some departments have gained extra time by asking students to undertake a preliminary unsupervised teaching practice in their home area either in July or in September. This has the advantage that the first term's course is unbroken, but it has the disadvantage that the department relies on the reports of schools rather than the first-hand experience of its own tutors in assessing the students' needs in the classroom. It also disturbs the arrangements made on an area basis for teaching practice. Some departments divide the teaching practice into two equal blocks of six weeks in consecutive terms, and some may even have only one or as many as three periods of teaching practice. Many departments have arrangements whereby much of the responsibility for the supervision of teaching practice is transferred to school tutors. But no department as far as is known departs very far from the principle that about one-third of the time is devoted to teaching practice and two-thirds to other aspects of the course.

Next, the proportion of the course devoted to method studies needs to be considered. There was a time when most departments

held one weekly meeting to discuss the methods of teaching each
subject, and little practical work was done. This arrangement has
been superseded in almost all departments by elaborate provision
for such work, especially in the sciences, in Fine Art and in languages, and more and more in geography, history and English,
until the time allotted can amount to half the theoretical part of
the course. Specialized rooms and equipment have been provided,
and the courses include discussion of the philosophy of each
subject and up-to-date studies of 'curriculum development' and
experimental syllabuses, demanding the provision and use of
course materials on a large scale. The expansion of this work raises
the problem of what proportion of time should be devoted to
it in an ideally arranged course—a question that is not easy to
answer.

Thirdly, work in educational studies needs to be considered.
Here the variety of arrangements in the different departments
draws attention to the problems. Since the course is 'initial'
training, how much of the rapidly expanding field of theoretical
studies in education can or should be included? How much
should be common to all students and what scope for choice should
there be? How much should be deferred until four or five years'
experience has been gained in the schools? The McNair Committee
considered that the course could be confined and many elements
postponed. But much has happened in the last twenty-five years
to make their view of the problem appear out of date. They were
no doubt over-optimistic about the proportion of graduate
teachers who would return to take diploma or higher degree
courses, though in recent years the growth-rate has increased.
But for many teachers the initial course of training will remain the
only substantial course in education they will take.

Faced with the difficulty of continuing to provide from two
to five basic elementary courses in education for all students,
covering (for example) the principles of education, the history
of education, educational psychology, social studies, and health,
which was at one time the common pattern, and which was
inevitably criticized for superficiality, the tendency has grown to
increase the number of courses, differentiating them and introducing a system of options. For instance, courses formerly known
as the principles of education tend to be broken down into
courses in educational philosophy, educational administration,
school organization, curriculum and examinations, and even into

much more specialized options on special subjects within these general fields. Similarly courses in educational psychology are broken down into sub-sections on child development, learning theory, mental testing, psychological theories, and so on. General courses in health (derived from the original 'hygiene' courses) have tended to disappear and to be replaced by specialized studies in the physiological aspects of child development, or to be absorbed into physical education courses taken by a minority of students. Social studies courses also have been differentiated into courses in educational sociology, aspects of social administration, and specialized courses in such topics as delinquency, educational priority areas, the education of immigrants and so on.

The solutions adopted by departments to the problems of organizing teaching in this complex field are various. Some retain a group of basic courses, with options added; some provide nothing but specialized courses, with guided choice by students; none, as far as is known, provide only the basic common courses, which twenty years ago were the convention. All undoubtedly feel that the growth of subject-matter needing attention makes it more and more difficult to rest content with the time available in the one-year course. The influence of the B.Ed. degree on the work of the departments needs to be mentioned. The syllabuses devised for the B.Ed. degree vary, as is by now notorious, from one university to another, but where, as is often the case, they are more ambitious than those in use in the university Departments of Education, the question inevitably arises whether the opportunities for educational study in an initial course of training should be more favourable for one class of student than for another.

Developments in examining in the departments over recent years have been away from the three-hour paper, which was the appropriate form of examining for the common lecture course, to the essay or written exercise which is a better way of examining more specialized courses. Experience has shown, however, that this system, which is scarcely the same as genuine 'continuous assessment', does not relieve the problem of the examining period in the summer which cuts off the course earlier than would otherwise be necessary.

One way of lengthening the course which has been suggested is to conclude with a period of teaching practice to coincide with the examination period: but unfortunately this involves the

schools in accepting students at a time when their own arrangements are abnormal because of examinations: although it is not
impossible to find useful work for students in schools at this time
of the year. We may conclude this part of the discussion of the
one-year course by observing that although some departments
make effective use of part of September and July none have fully
adopted the McNair suggestion.

We now need to consider various proposals that have been
made to improve the one-year course within the limit of one
academic year. Unfortunately most of these proposals have been
made by those who have had their eye on economic factors rather
than on the quality of the course. For instance it has been suggested
that the institution of an exacting vacation course of six or eight
weeks in August and September following graduation, followed
by teaching practice in the Michaelmas Term and a final term of
theoretical work in the Epiphany (Lent) Term, could produce a
trained graduate teacher by Easter. Such a course would have the
added advantage that it would make use of accommodation
which would normally be empty, and could be arranged to interlock with the present course. Another suggestion of the same
kind is that two or even three groups of students could be circu-
lated through the department and the schools in such a way that
the department building would be in permanent use and either a
half or a third of the students would always be on teaching
practice. (The implications of some of these schemes were examined
in a paper read to the Standing Conference on Studies in Education in 1962; see *B.J.E.S.*, May 1963.) Recently the Headmasters'
Association and Headmasters' Conference have issued a paper
advocating a variant of this kind in which half the students would
spend one term in schools and two in the department, while the
other half had only one term in the department and two in schools.
It is only fair to point out that this scheme also involved a preliminary vacation course and some 'day release' work in the
probationary year.

It is of course possible to lay down as a principle that the
building must always be in use by students taking postgraduate
initial courses of training and to explore the consequences of this
assumption. They seem to be that if half the time of all students
is to be spent on teaching practice, then two groups could alternate; if one third of the time of all students is to be spent on
teaching practice then three groups must rotate. If however

unequal periods of teaching practice are permissible, then two groups may alternate, one with one term of teaching practice and the other with two. If four terms were included in a year, which is essentially what would happen if the vacation course suggestion in the preceding paragraph were adopted, then two groups could alternate, each with two terms of teaching practice.

It is by no means clear, however, that any of these schemes, if confined to one year, would help to solve any of the problems which have been discussed above. Some of them would shorten the theoretical part of the course dramatically either for some or for all students. None would have any consequences which would *ipso facto* improve the course. They would present the department with the necessity of reorganizing its teaching *either* by dividing the staff as well as the students into two or three independent groups, *or* by instituting a system whereby all courses were repeated two or even three times *or* by abolishing timetabled teaching altogether and relying on individual work in consultation with staff supplemented by tutorial discussions. The first of these expedients would amount to the creation of two or more independent departments and would remove the benefit of increased size which would otherwise give all students access to a wider range of specialized teaching. The second expedient would be an unpleasant burden for the staff who teach large groups and would result in a wasteful use of staff for small-group teaching.

The third expedient perhaps merits further attention, since it has been the subject of at least one successful experimental course in a department, and is of course the basic idea of the Dalton Plan as it is carried out in certain schools. It raises the question of whether organized lecture courses are necessary or desirable in the teaching of education. If student-centred courses were developed and the emphasis were placed on individual reading and enquiry, with the staff of the department being available to provide discussion groups and individual tuition to guide the students' work, then organized timetables bringing together at one time all students interested in a given topic or all students who 'should' attend a lecture on a particular topic, would be unnecessary. Any grouping system could be adopted for alternating school practice and theoretical studies without adversely affecting the teaching. It should be pointed out, however, that such a system would on a rough calculation increase by almost 100 per cent the time spent by staff on teaching: though it would in compensation reduce considerably the time taken up in preparing and delivering courses of lectures. No one would think of such a far-reaching change in teaching simply in order to economize on the use of premises. But it deserves to be considered on its merits as a method that might produce better results and would certainly be consistent with some of the developments which are taking place in schools.

Tutorial teaching is already a strong component in most of the one-year courses, and many departments employ a system in which students have as many as three tutors, one for general discussions, one for school supervision and a third for method work or for seminars in educational studies. The change to a system which abolished lectures or reduced them to (say) one or two a week would not therefore be an adventure into entirely unfamiliar territory. Another aspect of tutorial teaching is the growing tendency for schools to appoint school-based tutors and for departments to employ teachers on short-term secondment as temporary (often part-time) tutors. This kind of arrangement serves to keep up a close relationship between work in the department and in the schools, and could if more fully developed help to reduce the gap which might otherwise exist between theoretical and practical work. It might even ease the situation by making it possible to transfer some method work into the school practice period. It is, however, impossible to envisage a substantial improvement of the one-year course by simple organizational manipulation. Most of the available variants have been tried at one time or another by one department or another, and the arrangements made are adjusted to the special situation in which the departments find themselves. Substantial changes are possible in the amount of participation in training by the schools, but there is little scope for improvement by the rearrangement of existing components. What matters is the individual student's work, and his growing understanding of the professional task he has undertaken through a sound interaction of theoretical studies and practical experience, both of which take time if they are to be thorough and significant.

The difficulties discussed above in the way of lengthening or improving the one-year course as it stands have led to exploration of possible forms of organization which go beyond the one-year pattern either back into the undergraduate years or forward into the early years of teaching service. As has been pointed out above, the four-year system which ended in 1951 had included in its earlier manifestations a certain amount of undergraduate teaching. Why did it break down? One reason was the overloading of students as the pressure of work in the degree courses increased; another was the inequality in the situation of the two groups of students, four-year and one-year; a third was the difficulty of making occasional courses and detached episodes of school practice really significant in a situation where educational studies were not a built-in part of the degree course.

One obvious course of action in recent years has therefore been to reinstitute the four-year course in a strengthened form within the degree course itself. Some university Departments of Education attempted to achieve this in their early days, but were unsuccessful. A fresh opportunity was presented by the creation of new universities. The Robbins Committee had spoken favourably of the idea, while the pioneer plan at Keele for a concurrent degree and diploma course had worked satisfactorily. The result was the development of undergraduate teaching of education in several other new universities in recent years. In a university where the structure of degree courses is being worked out from the beginning it is comparatively straightforward to timetable education as one of a range of subjects and to build it into a system of options in degree courses in arts, pure science or social studies. It is not so easy, though by no means impossible, in an established university with its timetables already congested, unless the assumption is made that 'Education students' will not want to take certain 'non-school' subjects against which education could be time-tabled. Such a restriction would be undesirable but might be necessary.

It is comparatively easy in a concurrent system to arrange short visits to schools as part of a course of studies, and to arrange for school investigations based on such visits, but it is more difficult to arrange school practice within the period spanned by the degree course. If courses were interrupted for a substantial period to enable students taking education to undertake school practice, how would the gap be filled for the students who were not taking education? Solutions to this problem were sought in Keele by having school practice in vacations, which placed a heavy burden on students. Former Colleges of Advanced Technology, using the

I

sandwich principle, have found it possible to adapt this system to contain teaching practice, but only where students are taking degree courses in which the sandwich principle is used in the students' other subjects. The University of York has solved the problem by confining the undergraduate studies in education to theoretical work, postponing teaching practice until the post-graduate year, which has been modified for those who have taken education as a degree subject.

There appear to be at least three ways in which degree courses could be arranged to include education with term-time teaching practice without difficulty. One is where the number of education students is so large that their work in other subjects can be economically arranged in separate classes, at least in the years in which teaching practice takes place, but it could well be argued that this would defeat the object of educating intending teachers alongside undergraduates with other vocational aims. A second is deliberately to omit parts of the syllabuses in other subjects which would then be taught in the absence of education students during teaching practice. This is unlikely to commend itself for a number of obvious reasons. A third is where, as at Cambridge, degree studies tend to be arranged consecutively, and an entirely self-contained full-time course in education, including an element of practical teaching, can be arranged.

Recent discussion of the possibility of a common two-year preliminary course in the universities has opened up the prospect of a consecutive pattern of studies within the degree course, the first stage being devoted to work in subjects other than education, the second, also of two years, to a professional course which might include not only education and practical teaching, but also valuable courses in which the educational implications of the subjects previously studied could be fully worked out. It should be noted, however, that this pattern and the consecutive pattern possible at Cambridge, really amount to transferring a whole year from the undergraduate course and adding it to the normal postgraduate year, and it is questionable whether the academic equipment of a student who took such a course would be as good as it ought to be.

In the case of the concurrent course proper, the arrangements can be much more flexible, the weighting of education studies can be varied from year to year, and the total time spent in the undergraduate years on such studies may be anything from a quarter to a half of the students' time. An important weakness of the concurrent course which it shares with the B.Ed. is that if the education and practical teaching component is more than one quarter of the whole then the comparatively short time devoted to the study of other subjects may affect the students' competence in those subjects in comparison with students who have taken a one-year consecutive training course. The major disadvantages of a concurrent course, however, as the colleges of education are finding out, is that it is incompatible with the postponement of a choice of career. It is possible to arrange it so that a choice is postponed until the second year, as happens at Keele; it is also possible to argue that the study of education is valuable for students irrespective of their career choice, but the fact remains that the purpose of the inclusion of such courses in the degree structure is to provide for the needs of those who intend to teach. The future of the concurrent course in the universities is therefore by no means secure.

As the discussion so far has made clear, the limitations of the one-year course made it inevitable that the possibility of prolonging it into the early years of teaching service should be investigated. In 1962 the Conference of Heads of University Departments of Education, in preparing evidence for the Robbins Committee, came to the conclusion that a proposal for two-year training with salaries instead of grants should be seriously made, and it was embodied in the conference's written evidence to the committee. The proposal was intended to serve four purposes: one was to improve the unsatisfactory nature of the probationary year, which had been the subject of many complaints; another was, by providing a more attractive course, to increase the number of graduate teachers entering the schools, and to reduce the tendency for them to enter the schools untrained (a tendency which has since to some extent been corrected); a third was to recognize the obvious fact that some of the best students from the university Departments of Education were giving such excellent service to the schools while on teaching practice that their contribution was indistinguishable from that of teachers in service, particularly untrained graduates in the early years of their work, who were being paid salaries instead of receiving grants; and the fourth was to satisfy the desire of the schools themselves that the proportion of time spent in training should be altered to provide longer experience in the schools, and to allow experienced teachers

to make a more valuable contribution to the training of recruits to
the profession.

It was considered that a two-year version of the postgraduate
course embodying the equivalent of two or three terms' theoretical
work and three or four terms' teaching experience, would also
have the following advantages. It would enable the whole course
to proceed at a more reasonable pace with more time for reading
and reflection, and would therefore make it more thorough; it
would provide more time either for theoretical studies or for
method work closely related to actual teaching or for both; it
would give the students longer in which to develop special investigations for their long essays or dissertations; it would not cost
much more than the present system and it might enable the
department buildings to be used at all times, since it would make
it possible for departments to design two interlocking variants of
the course. It would be a suitable course to institute as an alternative at the same time as a training requirement was introduced.

It was supposed that the reason why some students entered the
schools untrained was that they preferred not to take a course
which included a theoretical consideration of educational matters,
but an enquiry among untrained graduate teachers conducted in
1966 revealed that in all probability two-thirds at least chose not
to take a training course for other reasons, mainly financial.
However, the bias against theory was sufficiently substantiated to
justify a policy of offering certain courses in which the practical
component would occupy a larger proportion of the time than
is at present the case.

The Robbins Committee was occupied with more weighty
matters and did not recommend any changes in the arrangements
for training graduate teachers. The National Advisory Council
however had on several occasions recommended that training
should be made compulsory for graduates and while preparing
its Ninth Report published in 1965 it appointed a sub-committee
which unanimously and with the full support of the council
proposed a date (1969) for the introduction of a training requirement, having made some rough calculations of the number of
future training places which would be required. A further enquiry
by the Universities Council for the Education of Teachers into
the number of training places which would be needed was accepted
by the Department of Education and Science as a reasonably
accurate forecast and the government in 1969 finally committed

itself, announcing the introduction of a training requirement for graduates entering primary schools to operate from 1970, and for those entering secondary schools to operate from 1974. Those graduating in the years mentioned and in succeeding years would be subject to the training requirement.

This situation requires urgent action because the numbers coming forward for training will increase rapidly particularly from 1974 onwards, while a large number of graduates already in service and others not subject to the requirement will wish to obtain the basic teaching qualification. Proposals have been made by the Universities Council for the Education of Teachers to provide part-time versions of the training course for teachers in service, without the practical teaching component; and two versions of a modified course have been put forward for discussion. The present moment is therefore opportune for reviving the consideration of two-year alternatives to the present course in the hope that experiment will be encouraged and that variety of provision will be recognized from 1974 onwards.

There are a number of matters which arise when one is considering what kind of pattern to recommend for a two-year course. Several have arisen already in our consideration of one-year courses, and others need to be borne in mind. Of those already mentioned, it would seem desirable that a new type of course should provide opportunities for some students to take a more theoretically orientated course than others; it would seem desirable to devise a plan which would make the maximum use of department buildings; it would appear important to take advantage of the opportunity to involve teachers in the schools more fully than hitherto in training procedures, not at committee level alone, but in the actual teaching and supervision of students; and is clearly important that the pattern of alternation between school and department should provide substantial and effective periods of work in both, and that it should not unduly disturb the vacations of staff or students.

There are other important aspects to be considered. A new type of training course should not be much more expensive than the old, and should not make greater demands than the present arrangements do on members of staff, who are among the hardest worked of the university community. A new system must be simple and easy to understand and to administer. The financial conditions offered to students must be equitable, and therefore a system in which one group of students doing (say) a higher proportion of teaching in their course would be paid more than another group doing less teaching should be avoided. A new system must meet reasonable criticisms of the present course, as far as they are known, by both students and teachers, and must be acceptable to students doing both the B.Ed. course and the orthodox postgraduate course, who must regard it as no more advantageous financially than the course they are pursuing. These are not easy conditions to satisfy.

Very little is known of the views of students who have taken training courses about the value of the various components, though it is commonly said that they regard the teaching practice as of great value. A recent survey by the Headmasters' Association and Headmasters' Conference bears this out. Method courses are apparently appreciated, as are discussion group work and individual essay assignments. Theoretical work, presumably in lectures, is appreciated if it can be related effectively to contemporary and practical issues—in a word if it is 'relevant'. An enquiry addressed in 1966 to untrained graduate teachers—who of course knew of training courses only by hearsay—led to results which suggest that the three greatest needs are for (1) improved grasp of teaching method, (2) improved understanding of special subject method and (3) opportunities of practical teaching; while the next most important needs—but given half as much emphasis—are for (4) improved understanding of general theory of education, (5) better insight into children's behaviour and (6) fuller understanding of educational organization. There is little evidence here to justify the wholesale reduction of the theoretical element in training courses, but some justification for altering the balance so that the practical teaching and method components are extended.

The views of teachers, however, are reasonably well known. Some few of them take the view that the theoretical part of training courses is unimportant, but the majority consider that all teachers should be professionally trained, that there is a substantial theoretical component in a suitable course, but that a good deal more help can and should be given to students by properly constituted teacher-tutors working in the schools, in close association with training departments. This help is particularly required in connection with the day to day work of the schools, the details of classroom procedure, control of and relationship with children, and immediate matters of syllabuses, teaching materials, school administration and methods of examining.

These are very reasonable views, and they justify the inclusion in new plans for training of a better organized system of work by students in the schools. This cannot be satisfactorily achieved without substantially increased periods of school experience embracing the probationary year.

Before we consider possible arrangements for two-year courses, it is necessary to examine the administrative difficulties which they entail. A student under present arrangements spends his training year on a grant; school practice places are allotted to the department and the student is fitted into them as a supernumerary member of staff. If it is proposed that the first year of teaching service is to form part of the total pattern of training, then a student must be appointed to a school in the neighbourhood of the department, which has a working relationship with it: otherwise collaboration is impossible. It follows that some schools must be given the right by their L.E.A.s or governing bodies, to include in their establishment 'training places' for which salaries are paid, but which are occupied by trainee teachers, on a two-year contract of service, who would normally be expected to move to other posts for the third year, unless they were able to step into posts on the normal establishment of the 'training school' which happened to fall vacant at the right time. The contract would have to specify the amount of time to be spent in the school and in the department.

This conception is new in recent years, though in some respects it is not unlike a system which existed years ago in certain girls' secondary schools which trained teachers. It is not the same as the 'pupil-teacher' scheme though it has some common features. It would be necessary for the 'training schools' to appoint to vacancies for the two-year period students in degree courses, or in other employment, who wished to enter a 'two-year training course', and it would be necessary for the number of such vacancies in the schools in the area of a department to correspond with the number of vacancies in the department for two-year students. Unless these arrangements are made as a preliminary, the scheme would be unworkable. It is obviously necessary for schools undertaking these arrangements to have senior members of their staffs who are sufficiently free from normal teaching duties to make a considerable contribution to training in close collaboration with department tutors. It is also necessary for the school to devise ways, for example by pairing trainee teachers, or pairing them with students on teaching practice, to secure continuity of work during the absence of trainees at work in the department.

The remuneration of trainee teachers could be arranged either by paying a salary over the two-year period which would be equal to a grant plus allowances plus income tax added to a first-year salary, or by paying a grant for the first year and a salary for the second. A number of troublesome financial details like travelling expenses, university fees, union subscriptions and so on would have to be dealt with, and the dual status of the trainee as both a student and a teacher at the same time would have to be taken into account.

Given the feasibility of arrangements of this kind, we can go on to consider how suitable courses might be organized. One issue needs to be cleared up first: and that is whether or not it is desirable to use a two-year pattern in ways which would contribute to the economical use of buildings by the department. If it is, and if two-year training is to be organized side by side with one-year training, then possible arrangements are restricted. If two alternative types of two-year course are to be run at the same time, then they can be interlocked in such a way that more economical use of department buildings would result. A sound conclusion here would seem to be that courses should be judged on their own merits: if they interlock and can be staffed satisfactorily, so much the better. Another issue also needs to be considered: should vacations be used? A variant of the one-year course with an introductory session in the long vacation has already been discussed. Is it reasonable to ask a student to start work immediately after graduating? Many who have worked really hard for a final degree examination need rest, relaxation and outdoor exercise in the summer. It is, however, quite reasonable to ask that the course should begin with the opening of the school year. Vacation courses later on in the first or second year would seem also to be undesirable if the student is in fact working school-length terms. Next we need to consider whether day-release arrangements or evening work are appropriate. Here again there are difficulties. Students in schools at any considerable distance from a department (and there is no reason why distant schools should not participate in two-year schemes) would find both arrangements inconvenient. Evening work is in any case part of the teaching day for the conscientious teacher and part of the day's work for the serious student.

With these difficulties out of the way we can consider the basic possible alternations of periods of teaching and periods of study. First, however, we need to ask whether it is satisfactory to break the one-term unit down into periods of about six weeks. From the schools' point of view this is unsatisfactory, and it also tends to break the continuity of work in the departments. It is unavoidable in some situations in the one-year course, but is surely unnecessary in the ampler arrangements which a two-year course makes possible. We can therefore confine our attention to schemes which employ the whole term as a unit. If it is acceptable that some schemes should offer a higher proportion of theoretical work than others and that two terms is the minimum and three terms the maximum, the number of possible arrangements is limited. Table 10 would appear to exhaust all possible varieties except those with two consecutive terms of theoretical work.

Table 10. *Possible schemes for combining course work and teaching*

Terms		1	2	3	4	5	6
Scheme	[A	C	T	C /	T	T	T]
	B	C	T	C	T	C /	T
	C	C	T	C	T	T	C
	D	T	C	T	T	C /	T
	[E	T	C	T	C /	T	T]
	F	T	C	T	T	T	C
	[G	T	T	C	T	T	C]
	[H	T	T	C	T	C /	T]
	I	C	T	T	T	T	C
	J	C	T	T	T	C /	T
	[K	C	T	T	C /	T	T]
	L	C	T	T	C	T	C
	M	T	C	T	C	T	C

C = Course   T = Teaching

It would seem reasonable to eliminate A (which is the present one-year course), G and H, which require too much initial teaching and possibly E and K (which are four-term courses) but to retain B, D and J (which, though five-term courses, might be convenient). There seems no reason why a course should not be equally good if it begins and ends with either a term of theoretical work or a term of teaching. The remaining points on which the variants could be judged are (a) whether it is better to have a continuous run of teaching as in schemes F, I and J; (b) whether it is desirable to have two terms of theoretical work as in schemes D, F, I and J or three as in schemes B, C, L and M; (c) whether the weighting of theoretical work should be heavier at the beginning, as in B and C, or at the end as in L and M. It is difficult to see why all of the eight remaining schemes should not be available: B and C could conceivably be identical with a one-year course in the first year; the first term's work of I, J and L could be identical with that of a one-year course; D could interlock with two consecutive one-year courses; the first and second years of B could interlock with each other; and I could interlock with D.

The staffing implications of interlocking courses need to be examined, however. Such arrangements imply that the staff of the department will be teaching different groups in successive terms. This is no more difficult than teaching them in successive years, provided arrangements are made so that the staff are not required to spend a great deal of time in the same term both on visiting schools to supervise teaching practice, and on teaching in the department. The idea of interlocked courses under present teaching practice arrangements in the one-year course is ruled out for this reason, unless a new course is specially staffed. But under two-year arrangements, with school-based supervision of teaching practice, the possibilities become quite different. It is, however, arguable that the repetition of lecture courses twice a year, rather than annually, is tedious for staff, who with a year's interval are likely to revise lectures and bring them up to date. At this point, therefore, it is worth reconsidering whether re-structured training arrangements should not be based on a substantial reduction of lecturing and an increase of student-centred work based on assignments and tutorial supervision, with seminars and tutorial discussions replacing lectures. This, as was realized in our discussion of a different structure for the one-year course, would make work with alternating groups of students less uneconomical of staff time than would otherwise be the case, though the total use of staff time in teaching would undoubtedly increase. This however, in a school-based system, could be compensated for by a saving of the time (and travelling time) spent on visiting students, though not of course by its complete elimination.

The conclusion seems to be therefore that there is every reason why experiments with two-year school-based schemes should begin as soon as possible. One step could be taken which would release sufficient time to run them concurrently with the one-year course in the first instance: and that would be to make arrangements for much more school participation in the supervision of one-year students.

It is of course not inevitable that postgraduate courses of training would be improved if prolonged: it depends on whether structural alteration is accompanied by a new conception of the course. Anyone who is advocating a changed structure must meet the challenge of the sceptic who might ask what would be done with the extra time available. The proposals for a course consisting of two terms of theoretical work and four of teaching do not in fact lengthen anything but the teaching component: but a course with an extra term in the department lengthens both components. From the economic point of view a lengthened teaching component is paid for by service in the school: an additional theoretical component requires staffing, and it is proposed that it should be paid for by a shift of school practice supervision to the school, which would involve a slightly more generous staff establishment in the school. This has to be justified.

A teacher in training needs to have two 'workshops'. One must be in the school, where his ideas about how to organize and present subject-matter, how to arrange children's work, how to develop a successful working relationship with children and colleagues, how to play his part in the administrative tasks which fall to all teachers, are put to the test of practical experience. In addition he learns in the same workshop to play his part in school social and extra-curricular activities and games.

The other 'workshop' needs to be outside the school in an atmosphere of specialized study and enquiry, among people who have devoted their lives to the study of education and related subjects, but who have not lost touch with the schools, whose teaching can illuminate some of the practical problems that arise in the schools, but can also help the student to work out a professional philosophy, and to inform himself about the theoretical implications of children's development and of the educational system and its procedures, so that his judgments may be sound and sensible and his interests may transcend the immediate practical issues that arise in his day to day work.

A glance at what happens to some students (the least fortunate no doubt) suggests that the school 'workshop' can be improved, but it cannot be substantially improved in the short periods of school practice at present available. Many students say of their teaching practice that they are withdrawn from it when they feel that they are beginning to develop confidence and mastery and to form a good relationship with children. Others find a conflict between the views of the staff of the school and those of the staff of the department, which could be reduced or eliminated by a planned relationship between the two groups of staff. In the one-year course this tends to be left to chance—in a longer course in which the aim would be more ambitious it could not be treated in this way. Opinion both in the schools and in the departments is moving to a position in which there would be much goodwill devoted to the working out of an improved version of the school 'workshop'.

What would happen to the department 'workshop'? Here at the moment there is great hurry and pressure. Initial briefing of students has to be conducted in haste; schools complain that students arrive unprepared; method courses try to cover what all students in the subject may need for their next teaching practice, while at the same time the foundations are laid for specialized courses which need considerable reading if they are to be mastered. This work is interrupted for the vacation and a further teaching practice and is then resumed after Easter in another rapid series of courses which are prematurely concluded in order to hold an examination or collect and assess the written work which has been done. There are normally two continuous threads—the chain of preparation for teaching and the chain of written assignments— with perhaps also a connected series of tutorial discussions—and the development of the study of education over a continuous period is extremely difficult and contrasts unfavourably with the atmosphere of undergraduate courses. The remarkable thing is that from the best students so much is achieved in so short a time.

A redesigned system planned so that no course is less than a term in duration, with examinations or work assignments placed so far ahead that thorough preparation is possible and time is available for a long series of evenings, weekends and vacations for reading and following up ideas, would |restore confidence and make the department 'workshop' a genuine academic institution with its resources fully used. It is true that the plans discussed above involve breaks in the continuity of attendance at the department—(schemes involving two consecutive terms of theoretical work could be added to the list although they have been omitted at this stage)—but the opportunity would exist to contruct a programme with continuous reading and enquiry extended over the periods of teaching.

The ideal system obviously does not exist, but a whole term's work *preceding* teaching experience could contain a much more thorough method of preparation and examination of syllabuses than is possible at present, with school-orientated studies supplementing it, while the more theoretical studies could be deferred until the second term of theoretical work, to be carried to a more advanced stage in a third term, in the case of students who had chosen the more theoretically orientated course. Meanwhile the momentum given to the method studies and school-orientated studies could be carried forward by the school-based work in the intervening terms in a planned sequence, agreed between school and department tutors.

It is perhaps appropriate to conclude with a diagrammatic presentation of a possible course, based on Scheme L assuming teaching practice to take place in a comprehensive school. It is assumed that this type of course would achieve first degree standard in education.

First Term in Department

*1   Method studies in general and in separate branches of the curriculum (including a short period of observation and teaching).
*2   Special subject method courses, including curriculum development and mixed ability group teaching.
3   The elementary theory and practice of examining.
4   Educational structure and recent history.
5   School organization, including school visits.

* Related to teaching programmes planned for second and third terms.

6 Special subjects (including provision for the handicapped) within the general field of curriculum and method with opportunities for individual investigations.

Second and Third Terms in School

1 A gradually increased timetable in students' special subjects, syllabuses and level of work chosen to relate to the special subject method work (2 above).
2 Opportunity to study the structure and organization of the school, its environment, and its place in the educational system, its staffing, its policy and principles, its system of government and the work of the local education authority, including the social, psychological and careers advisory services, and the health service available to children.
3 Opportunity to take part in a wide variety of school activities.

Fourth Term in Department

1 More advanced study of school organization and curricula' and comparative study of different educational institutions·
*2 Futher enquiry into method, syllabuses, especially in integrated courses, and experimental teaching in special subjects and with special groups.
3 Introductory studies in psychology and child development, with systematic study of examining and testing techniques.
4 Introductory studies in educational philosophy or history.
5 Introductory studies in sociology of education or educational administration or comparative education.
6 Special subjects leading to essays and special enquiries.

Fifth Term in School

1 A full timetable resumed with opportunities for experimental work.
2 Opportunity for work with special groups (e.g. remedial classes—one or more examination classes at various levels— related to work done in 2 and 3 above) and in integrated courses.
3 Opportunity to use school resources for completion of special enquiries (begun in 6 above).

* Related to teaching programme planned for fifth term.

Sixth Term in Department

1 Further studies in psychology with assignments of work drawing on school experience and on fourth term courses and reading.
2 Further studies in educational philosophy or history with either essays or a dissertation.
3 Further studies in sociology of education or educational administration or comparative education, with essays.
4 Opportunity to complete either essays or dissertation on special enquiries initiated in fourth term.

Final assessment.

The relationship of such a course to in-service training would be that, having reached first degree standard in initial training, those wishing to pursue further studies in education could proceed direct to the higher degree by course and examination or by thesis without an intermediary diploma stage. One of the problems of the present provision of in-service work for graduates is that is is assumed (probably correctly) that their one-year course of training does not take them to first degree standard; and the more closely the course is related to their immediate needs in the school practices the more correct this assumption is. There should be opportunities for graduates in subjects other than education to attain a higher standard in educational studies than is at present possible and this is the justification for the reorganized course including three terms of theoretical work.

Eight

Brian Cane

In-Service Education for Teachers

In-service education is a fashionable topic for the educational agenda. Official and semi-official pronouncements on education set out the arguments for reform in this or that area of teaching and invariably end by stressing the need for an immediate expansion of in-service provision so that teachers can up-date themselves, and become adequately primed for reorganization and curriculum innovation. In these reports, there is a tacit acceptance of the argument that the needs of the schools have long ago outpaced the time-scale of conventional teaching training: the working life of a teacher is seen to encompass not one, but a host of major revolutions in educational practice, so that pre-service teacher education cannot provide more than an introduction to professional work. The corollary of this popular viewpoint is that the practising teacher must accept study and experiment as part of his normal duties.

But how is this aspect of the teacher's role to be realized? It is not sufficient that many professors of education and D.E.S. staff have come to recognize the need: frequently one hears the view that the pre-service component of teacher education should constitute a much smaller proportion of the total quota of teacher education to be provided by the state—indeed the *avant-garde* among the mandarins are suggesting the proportion might be less than one half. Yet a proportion of 5 to 10 per cent remains in many localities a pious intention: recent reports have exposed the gross inadequacy of both content and arrangements in most areas of the country, and at most levels of training. The provision is frequently piecemeal and unco-ordinated, and one can point to just a few geographical locations or subject areas for which the provision is promising.

A preliminary in the discussion of this topic must be the definition of the term 'in-service teacher education'. Formal courses are frequently considered to be the chief component, but increasingly other forms of in-service work are thought of as contributing to the teacher's professional education and development: among these activities are the working parties, study groups, development projects and examination committees that meet locally, regionally and nationally. It seems essential to have a flexible definition if we are not to pre-judge the issue before we start our discussion. Hence, in-service teacher education is taken to include all those courses and activities in which a serving teacher may participate for the purpose of extending his professional knowledge, interest or skill. Preparation for a degree, diploma or other qualification, subsequent to initial training would be included within this definition.

In the N.F.E.R. survey, conducted three years ago, 80 per cent of teachers declared positively their need for in-service training (broadly defined), yet between one-sixth and one-quarter of experienced teachers had not taken any form of training whatsoever, and most of the remainder had participated in only one or two courses or working parties, often of very brief duration. In one northern county, 49 per cent of all teachers had taken no in-service training at all, and this fact underlines the unevenness of provision. Half the teachers from different counties who had been to courses or joined professional groups evaluated the experience as of little benefit to their teaching, and a similar proportion declared that there was a shortage of the kind of in-service education that they wished to attend. Their dissatisfaction was borne out by an analysis which showed that little if any L.E.A. course time was given to four of the nine topics in most demand by teachers, and that arrangements for courses were generally not those most favoured by teachers.

Surveys such as this underline the need for considerable modification and expansion in the programmes now operated by the D.E.S., L.E.A.s and university institutes, involving not only changes in policy and organization, but also different priorities and allocations of resources. Until fundamental strategic issues are faced, the growth in in-service teacher education must remain stunted and uneven, and comments on possible future patterns for development must have a discouragingly speculative flavour. Therefore, any discussion of the future pattern over the next thirty to forty years must first explore some of the important general issues that need airing: the logistic plan that follows this exploration is put forward as one possible solution—a basis for further consideration.

The Americans have a habit of listing the cardinal principles that must be the keystone of some new educational programme. This habit is useful in that it helps to ensure that the programme proceeds in a balanced manner, and has a positive dynamic from

K

the start. The basis of action is highlighted from the beginning.
Adopting this mode, we might postulate the following cardinal
principles for action in in-service teacher education:

Cardinal Principles for Action

  1 In each locality, there must be a systematic, continuing and
objective assessment of the need and the demand;
  2 In each locality, there must be effective consultation with
teachers in every type of school and college;
  3 The existing Area Training Organization structure for
teacher education must be reformed drastically, if not replaced by
a new structure;
  4 In-service education must be voluntary, but defined so that
it is more closely related to named qualifications;
  5 Teaching must become an all-graduate profession;
  6 Educational research and development must be totally integrated with in-service teacher education;
  7 A new type of regional university must emerge, representative of teachers in an area, and centred on colleges of education:
this radical innovation in British higher education would parallel,
but be quite different from traditional universities and polytechnics.
  These 'principles' will be discussed in turn. No doubt there
are some other principles that might be considered: the seven
listed above have a coherent relationship, and provide a foundation
that can be challenged or extended by colleagues.

The assessment of need and demand

It might seem unnecessary to stress that in-service teacher education should be attuned to the needs of the schools and the circumstances of teachers. The fact is that until recently little attempt
was made to ensure that it was! We do not seek the edification of
teachers in a Spencerian fashion, with the accent on knowledge
for its own sake or the 'good' professional cast in a single mould.
The chemistry teacher will pursue the study of recent advances
in his subject, not principally because he is interested, but rather
as a means to reviewing the order and content of the subject-
matter and experimental work that he teaches in the classroom.
Likewise, the primary teacher will study advances in psychology
or sociology, for instance, because ultimately she is concerned

with the improvement of school practice, not because the academic knowledge acquired is an end in itself.

The priorities for in-service education will vary from one locality to another, and from one level of schooling to another. Methods of assessing the demand are generally haphazard and unreliable at present. So often, the organizer of a course or a working party takes a stab in the dark and hopes that there will be a response both to the subject and the arrangements made. In future, there must be systematic regional and local market research, preferably organized by the authorities but independently carried out. This research might be organized periodically, say every two years, as part of the normal routine of teaching. It should be so conducted that it would uncover specific requirements and weaknesses. It could be linked to a parallel review of the requirements locally for educational research and development.

At present, the requirements are defined separately by the staff of Institutes of Education, Local Authority Advisors, D.E.S. Inspectors, and to some extent, by officers of professional associations or institutes. Most of these groups tend to operate alone, sometimes with disastrous results in terms of overlap and balance between one type of course and another. We must face the fact that there are wide variations in the extent and nature of provision in different Institutes of Education and different local authorities, and that these give rise to many more deficiencies than can be accepted in a coherent national programme.

The comparison has to be made to be believed. Why should probationers be ignored in the in-service programme of one county, while in another county or county borough several advisors, a university institute, and a college of education, combine to help probationers through the difficult initial year of teaching? Why should religious education be ignored as a topic for in-service activity by many counties and area training organizations, yet be considered so important in another county that it merits a specialist advisor and courses for *all* primary teachers in the area? Why should part-time diploma courses or part-time B.Ed. degree work be available in a few university institutes, but not in others, and why is the range of courses available often so limited? Leading questions of this kind could fill the rest of this chapter. The excuse presented is generally that financial resources are quite inadequate: I remain unconvinced that this difficulty is the sole stumbling-block, otherwise the provision would be at the same uniform minimum throughout the country.

Procedures and structures are at least as important as finance. The demonstrated inadequacy of provision raises questions that require immediate attention. How should the need and the demand be defined, and by whom? Can we rely alone upon the wisdom of hard-pressed individuals—the local administrators, the institute directors, the wardens of teacher centres? Market surveys will help, using both interviews and questionnaires, but in addition we need effective mechanisms for consultation with the teaching profession (including associated professionals), and this may not be possible within existing organizational structures.

Consultation with teachers

This problem suggests at once that the geographical area for co-ordination needs careful attention. Consultation cannot occur remotely, or within enormous units. A unit of 300 or 400 primary schools and 100 secondary schools is probably too large. The maximum proportion might be no greater than twenty-five secondary schools and seventy-five to one hundred primary schools. Smaller units might be the basis for organizing short courses. Clusters of three or four of such units might form the hinterland for part-time courses in preparation for named qualifications, but the consultation and organization would still be effected through the smaller units.

The professional associations might be given a more dynamic and challenging role than hitherto. The one-off local jamboree, or the summer school of yesteryear, are probably no longer appropriate. The activities of professional associations could be integrated into the local in-service programmes in new ways. Representation of teachers on consultative groups could be by election from the whole teaching body in the unit, not by nomination from professional associations. The role of the associations would then be that of pacemaker and watchdog, and they would nominate observers to co-ordinating groups not representatives. We thus arrive at the notion of a local 'College of Teachers'—a united, professional and non-partisan body. The in-service providing bodies might be responsive to the needs as expressed and ascertained by this 'college', without necessarily foregoing any independence in terms of authority or control.

The concept of staffs of schools and colleges being an integral part of a complete regional system of education is not new. The idea was developed by Diderot in France in the eighteenth century, although not in precisely the form suggested now. Diderot's concept was extended to America by Jefferson in 1779; he incorporated the French concept in his abortive plan for the 'University of Virginia'. More successful was a further American adaptation, 'The University of the State of New York', which embraced institutions at primary, secondary and tertiary levels. The 'University Michigania', formed in 1817, had a similar basis. Later the American State universities formed in the middle and far west promoted close links between schools and colleges.

What is needed for the future of British education is a refinement and development of this approach, which does not contain the seeds of its own collapse: in a sense, the Area Training Organization was a brave attempt to introduce a closer relationship between schools, colleges and university, but we must admit that in most A.T.O.s the attempt failed during the fifties and sixties largely because the training colleges and university departments of education were insufficiently developed to provide either the leadership required or the services for research and in-service training. The establishment of pre-service education at the first degree level has preoccupied the A.T.O.s and monopolized most of the resources.

The re-constitution of Area Training Organizations

The next two decades might bring a broadening out from the pre-service programme to include strong research centres or units such as already exist in embryo at London, Bristol, Manchester and Birmingham. The research facility will be integrated with the in-service, higher degree and diploma work. But if this work is to be closely associated with all teachers and schools in the vicinity, the A.T.O.s must disappear in their present form and structure. Not only will they place less emphasis on pre-service education, but they will be different in geographical area, probably centred on colleges of education instead of a traditional university, with some additional colleges deliberately founded in localities at present isolated from a centre of learning and research. Eventually, one might envisage the constitution of colleges designed to fulfil this role as changing to the extent that they become part of, rather than continue separate from, the teaching profession in the schools.

As a move in this direction, we might hope that a larger number of practising teachers might be invited to sit on the governing bodies of both colleges of education and schools. Likewise, in many areas a conscious effort might be made to persuade College staff to serve as governors of schools. Teachers and advisory staff might be invited to attend meetings of college academic boards, and the agenda might include other business than the immediate questions arising from the organization of pre-service education, for instance, local curriculum development, research projects, reorganization etc. College staff might attend school staff meetings and meetings of the L.E.A. advisory staff. Again, this kind of consultation would not be possible unless the unit of college-schools-L.E.A. was carefully defined and considered, but it is towards this kind of working relationship and understanding that we must work.

Compulsory or voluntary participation?

Pre-service education for teaching is compulsory now, and the arguments for such compulsion can be applied just as readily to in-service teacher education. The State must be concerned that minimum levels of professional competence are maintained: minimum competence in a rapidly changing society covers more than a functional capability, but must include an up-to-date knowledge of content and methods. One could make a strong case for compulsory in-service training on the basis that professional practice changes so rapidly that we must ensure that *all* teachers renew their skills and knowledge. We could go as far as proposing re-qualification every ten years.

Yet the implementation of such a proposal would be fraught with dangers. On the one hand, the inspectorate might return to their old assessment role, with a consequent loss of advisory activities. A monstrous apparatus for periodic examination by written papers or vivas might engulf us, so that teaching was further constrained by a straitjacket of examination practices. Clearly, only a small minority is likely to favour absolute compulsion: the price paid would be considered too great by most teachers.

Those disliking compulsion fear an interference with their

professional independence and autonomy; they may also fear the imposition of a rather rigid and ineffective 'official' programme of in-service courses, over which they would have little control. The 1967 N.F.E.R. Survey found that many teachers considered that the devotion and enthusiasm of teachers was underestimated, and that there was a lot of evidence that teachers would attend in-service education programmes without any strings attached.

There are many degrees and shades of compulsion, and there is a fair amount of 'compulsory' in-service training accepted by teachers. Courses that are stipulated by employers with impending reorganization in mind, or perhaps in reaction to some local social problem, are not generally boycotted: the acceptance of such compulsion is only partly explained by the fact that the courses take place in school time.

Many teachers, especially in primary schools, felt that authorities should encourage attendance through a scheme that links attendance to promotion possibilities. Opposition comes from other teachers who fear that such a scheme might lead to unacceptable practices. They view with distaste the 'course mongerers': they are suspicious of the professional aims of teachers that attend courses that facilitate promotion. One Surrey teacher said that 'too many teachers go to too many courses for the wrong reasons ... all too frequently they pursue promotion or are dodging the day-to-day classroom work'. In some counties today, the in-service training record of teachers *is* noted by interviewing committees, and may even have a place on the application form.

The danger is that the connections between course attendance and promotion prospects are not always clearly understood. The requirement of qualifications for certain posts is compelling, but at least everyone shares the knowledge that these qualifications will be a minimum requirement. It may be healthier for a profession to have a form of compulsion that is open, declared and well defined, rather than made up from casual intelligence, patronage or even hidden canvassing. In this sense, there is probably a majority of teachers in favour of linking more in-service work to named qualifications, provided these qualifications can be earned in convenient ways and for work that is related to school practice.

Whilst some Surrey teachers seemed suspicious of attempts to link training with promotion prospects, there was no apparent opposition to publicized links between in-service training and salary additions. In the view of several teachers, the question of how this might be done required a great deal more thought and attention. Attendance at long-term courses, involving considerable sacrifices of personal time and expense, and culminating in a final examination, was considered to be deserving of a prize in the form of salary additions. But many teachers in the survey were not so certain that short, unexamined courses or activity could earn similar recognition on a basis acceptable to all. It was suggested that the American credit system be adopted, and that points earned for attendance should qualify a teacher for extra increments, but others considered that the totting up of attendances would take away all the joy and pleasure from in-service training.

This discussion suggests that the future pattern of in-service teacher education will retain the voluntary aspect, but there will be a development of local part-time/full-time courses leading to named qualifications and recognized nationally for additional increments of salary. The teaching profession will become more closely involved in the control of these courses, which will be offered in short units as well as in long units. Completion of work for research and development projects, and other forms of school-based training, will increasingly contribute to the award of these qualifications. This development will intensify the problems of accreditation for institutions awarding the qualifications, and may mean that colleges of education should become award-giving bodies in their own right.

An all graduate profession?

Professional people are those whose practice requires high-level skills and a long period of education: they control the standard of entry to their profession, and determine the accepted code of professional conduct. It does not follow that the professional education needs to be part of a university programme, but with the development of British technological universities, colleges of education with honours degree students, and polytechnic students taking C.N.A.A. degrees, we have seen a new move towards the incorporation of more professional education within the university orbit.

This trend has both a credit and debit side for the professional. On the credit side, his education is associated more closely with systematic research in his area of professionalism—or it should be.

The advantages of this connection are clear in professions like medicine. We have little reason to doubt that they could be equally important to the teaching profession, unless we doubt the value of applying the methods of research in, say, history, philosophy or social science, to the practice of education. But, on the debit side, the more teacher education becomes a university concern, the more danger there is that professional control of this education will weaken. The L.E.A.s have seen this danger: have the teachers?

The signs are that we must expect an all-graduate profession to be nearly established by 1985. The pre-service programmes may have changed so that the present certificate qualification becomes regraded as a pass degree, and the four-year course for an honours B.Ed. degree will be taken by at least one-third of all college students, perhaps more. The present trends suggest that more college entrants will have matriculation qualifications at entry. By 1980, colleges will have introduced more diploma courses, and will be offering higher degree courses linked to research units: at least 10 per cent of college students will postpone teaching to take a higher degree at college.

The seventies will show a rapid establishment of the in-service B.Ed. degree, with colleges giving over 10 per cent or more of their teaching to full-time, or part-time courses. These courses may not only be associated with the local university, but also with the Open University and with the C.N.A.A. Part-time provision is likely to overshadow the full-time provision, with a tendency to emphasize service to the local catchment area within a radius of fifty miles of the college. The colleges that can adapt to this pattern through the introduction of evening and vacation courses will forge new links with the local teachers.

Eventually, perhaps during the period 1980-5, the demand for these in-service B.Ed. degree courses will slacken as most newly qualified teachers graduate from college with first degrees. The eighties will see a rise in demand for facilities for research and for higher degree provision. It will be at this stage that the challenge to traditional structures for the organization of higher education will become most intense. By the eighties, it is essential that a new framework for teacher education shall have emerged—a framework which will facilitate realistic, school-based training and research for every locality. To effect this, the seventies must bring the restructuring of A.T.O.s already suggested, and at the same time, there must be a great leap forward in research methods, especially evaluation techniques.

The teaching profession and the authorities must wake up to the urgency of the matter now. We should recognize the importance of building now the sound foundation on which future investigations will depend. The National Foundation for Educational Research must be expanded during the seventies and invited to place more emphasis on the construction of new research instruments, basic design and analysis procedures, as well as the techniques of school and classroom observation. More evaluation projects should be funded so that the essential experience with new techniques can be obtained. Both the Schools Council and the N.F.E.R. should be asked to seek local bases for projects, and to co-operate in forming diploma and M.Sc. courses in educational research and development. The D.E.S. and the S.S.R.C. should develop a coherent policy in this direction immediately, and earmarked funds should be directed to those colleges and universities that are willing to take the initiative in setting up research units with permanent staffs and services.

Ten years is a short time in educational history. There is real danger that the accelerating production of first education graduates will generate a demand for research and post-graduate programmes before there has been an adequate development of research methodology and services. If this happens, we may get a repetition in Britain of the false scholarship in education that has been evident in some higher institutions in America. We still have time to avoid this situation, which would lead ultimately to a lowering in quality of schooling in this country. But the early seventies must see a sense of urgency about this problem, especially amongst those who control funds for research. There is no doubt in my mind that recent years have witnessed a drying up of funding for what I would call fundamental educational research. We cannot allow this policy to continue.

In-service education and research or development

In any case, improvements in professional standards will depend on continued experiment, investigation, research and development, alongside a vigorous programme aimed at applying, evaluating and communicating the skills and knowledge thus gained. Already a chief function of in-service education is to communicate and explain these advances. The considerable interest in the writings of Miss Biggs on primary-school mathematics, and of Dr Joyce Morris on primary-school reading, demonstrates the value of this function. Seventy per cent of teachers in Durham, Norfolk and Glamorgan in the 1967 N.F.E.R. Survey wanted short courses on the results of educational research relevant to their own work.

In the 1968 N.F.E.R. Study, 'The teacher and research', many teachers emphasized that for them the involvement in research projects was itself a training experience. However fruitful in terms of results a project might be—and not all projects can be exciting in that sense—the greatest success may come indirectly through giving the participating teachers the opportunity to think more deeply and critically about their classroom work and professional beliefs. One project may not answer many questions, but it may stimulate an awareness of possibilities and trigger off further research which might itself be of the greatest significance. Involvement in research is a means of breaking down the teacher's working isolation, and a chance to tackle problems with colleagues from one's own and other schools.

These conclusions suggest that it would be positively advantageous if in-service education and research/development were organized and developed together on a local and regional basis. Should we consider the planning, funding and organization of research and development alongside that of in-service education? Should there be a major policy decision to integrate the two? Such a decision need not necessarily threaten the position of the full-time researcher: indeed the need for fundamental research would become even greater, and full-time appointments would increase in number.

The implications of such a policy are numerous, not least that the funding of research would include a conscious consideration of in-service education for every project involving teachers. Ultimately, this might mean that the Schools Council might be disbanded in its present form: instead, regional equivalents would organize projects integrated with in-service programmes, and apply to the central agency for specific assistance. Initiatives would be taken by the regional bodies, and the old Schools Council would become a service centre responding to requests. A good proportion of the monies previously channelled through the Schools Council for development projects would be handed to the regional bodies instead. Likewise, the service functions of the N.F.E.R. would be developed as an aid to regional research projects, and the Foundation would provide co-ordinating functions as appropriate, especially for evaluation work.

The policy of integrating research and in-service education might lead to other changes of emphasis in research planning. Good ideas would be seen to be insufficient as a basis for development work. Instead, there would be more reliance on research that studied teachers at work, and schools or systems in operation. What are the objectives of the teacher in action? How do the schools differ one from another in terms of professional practice and belief? What are the practices which make for most success (according to defined criteria) in the *observed* circumstances of classroom or school?

We cannot pretend to have made much progress with studies designed to investigate these questions. A few studies point the way, for instance the N.F.E.R. 'French in primary schools' project, or the N.F.E.R. 'Teaching beginners to read' project. The recent N.F.E.R. 'Teaching day' project demonstrates the relevance of these empirical studies, both to the practice of teaching and the content of teacher education. Thomas Huxley used to say: 'Sit down before fact like a little child.' We have hardly begun this empirical observational stage in educational research, yet observational work may be as important to education as to the sciences. There is little doubt in my mind that extensive and objective studies of schools/systems in operation could lead to radical changes, not least in the management of teaching.

A new type of university?

It is arguable that, in their haste to achieve traditional university status, the technological universities—and perhaps in their turn the polytechnics—will have missed the opportunity to create a fresh concept and structure for a university. The nature of a university has changed through the ages, but there has always been an emphasis on the education of the professions, and the extension of knowledge through research. The weakness of British universities in their response to modern conditions is that their functional links with the professions have been tenuous, and that their service functions to the *local* communities have been much less developed than in some other countries. Could we not conceive of a new kind of 'professional university' that stressed these latter features?

Given that the trends discussed in this chapter had borne fruit by the nineteen-eighties, it might be possible to detach the Schools of Education and Area Training Organizations from existing universities of the traditional kind and to form them into new 'university-type' institutions to be known as 'professional universities'. I refer to 'university-type' institutions because although I reckon that these 'Universities of Professionals' will perform the chief functions of universities today, namely research and teaching at the highest levels, I do not feel that the Oxbridge-Redbrick pattern, or the polytechnic pattern, are the kind to be applied. I would like a new type of institution that may be applicable to the needs of school-teaching alone: I would hesitate to judge whether it was relevant to the needs of other professions, but it might well be; if so, there might be a case for parallel 'Universities of Professionals'.

This new kind of university would conduct research and degree work in a number of disciplines: it would constitute a community of students and scholars, but their chief concern would be the quality and effectiveness of teaching at all levels in the state system of education, instead of the advance of knowledge in a particular subject area, or the development of a particular technology such as civil engineering. A 'University of Teachers' would be established in each regional area of the country—say ten or twelve in all. Each would be unique in that they would be seen to embrace all teachers within a geographical region, full membership being granted to all graduate teachers, and associate-ship membership to non-graduates. Thus, convocation for such institutions would have a reality that escapes the postal fiction of many existing universities. The senate would include the leaders of education in the regional community. Funding for pre-service and in-service teacher education, as well as for regional educational research and development, would come from a national 'Professional Universities Grants Committee' separate from those concerned with traditional universities.

It is a fair argument that the development of schools has been proscribed for the last 150 years by a particular pattern for higher education. In Britain, the traditional universities have largely determined the curriculum and examinations of secondary schools, and teachers have had less say in the process than is consistent with full professional responsibility. The teacher is the key to educational progress, and advances in the schools depend on teachers having greater professional freedom, more expertise and more status. They cannot be fully professional if they are effectively constrained within a traditional system dominated by a university structure that is in many ways inappropriate and not closely linked with the practice of teaching. These arguments suggest that the 'professional university' for teachers should become the third force in British higher education which could allow the expansion in numbers required without damaging the ethos of existing universities. Indeed, it may be that the way ahead for British higher education, is to allow the new-type universities to take over and extend all general first degree courses (both honours and pass), and to develop research and higher degree work of a distinctively professional kind, whilst the traditional universities concentrate on the specialist first degree courses, and the specialist research and higher degree work in the single subject disciplines.

The transition period

Changes in British education are generally suspect until they can be demonstrated as effective and necessary. The seventies may form a period of transition towards the kind of future for teacher education that I have pictured. During this transition period, certain aspects will be tested and structures modified. There is a danger that the balance of provision for in-service education will swing too far towards short courses for all teachers. Our first priority is to ensure that we have a good flow of well-qualified leaders in the teaching profession. This means that we must expand the provision for named qualification courses, and ensure that the provision is adequate and even everywhere in the country.

(a) *Named qualifications*

National surveys have shown that the demand for B.Ed. degree courses will be such that approximately one-quarter to one-third of the existing teaching force today will want to take the degree if arrangements are convenient. This means that the initial response will be very great in most localities, as indeed the Lancaster programme has shown. The demand is likely to increase as more teachers realize the importance of graduate status, and the rewards to be obtained; but, in my view, the size of the response will depend on whether the universities make convenient arrangements for part-time study, and the extent to which universities accept each other's initial teacher qualifications as a fulfilment for matriculation and for part one of the degree programme. There is a strong case for a uniform policy, but where universities fail their local teachers we must expect to see the Open University or the C.N.A.A. filling the gap.

It is inevitable that the colleges of education will be the main centres for the in-service B.Ed. degree course. They alone have the facilities, outlook and locations required. The pressure will be severe in centres of concentrated urban development. What will be the likely extent of this in-service development in colleges of education? A D.E.S. estimate was based on the assumptions that only three-year trained teachers in the age range twenty-five to forty-five years would be interested, and that married women with family responsibilities would opt out: on this basis, the maximum number of serious candidates in the present work force was thought to be 14,000. However, one university is already offering an in-service B.Ed. to teachers of twenty-three years of age, and there seems no reason to expect a teacher with at least ten years of service left not to consider the possibility of a B.Ed. course part-time. Married women returners may be among the first to seek up-dating in the form of a deferred B.Ed. programme. The evidence of the two national surveys in 1967 suggested that 90,000 to 120,000 teachers of all ages and circumstances would be responsive to local courses for B.Ed. Now that the B.Ed. pre-service provision is gathering momentum, the number of serving teachers seeking the B.Ed. qualification is likely to increase. All this suggests that the D.E.S. estimate of 14,000 was a gross underestimate. It seems likely that colleges will have to provide for at least as many in-service B.Ed. students as they have pre-service B.Ed. students at present: in large colleges, this may be as many as 300 students taking a three-year part-time course (bridging year plus two-years' B.Ed. work).

It is a safe assumption that the number of students in pre-service teacher education will not decrease during the next decade. Therefore, college staffing and facilities must expand by anything up to 25 per cent in order to cope with the pressure from serving teachers for the B.Ed. qualification. Many who take university diploma courses at present may prefer the B.Ed. courses in

future, but there will be a continuing demand for diploma courses
—indeed, the demand is likely to increase as the need to be better
qualified becomes more evident and insistent. Many graduates
will take specialist courses. Many non-graduates will seek the
university diploma as a terminal qualification, or as a means of
proving their suitability to be admitted to a degree course. In
some universities, the diploma may be stipulated as a requirement
for entry to a higher degree by thesis. It must be remembered
too that a diploma qualification earns an addition to the salary
scale. For all these reasons, we may expect an expansion in the
number of students in diploma courses by a factor of five or more
over the next decade. On economic grounds, it would be most sensible for this expansion to take place again in the colleges, so that by
1980 colleges would range in size from 1,000 to 2,000 students or
more, with perhaps one quarter of their students taking part-time/
full-time in-service B.Ed. degree or diploma courses. The most
viable of these courses would be the part-time provision.

With this kind of development, a major question is the relative
roles of colleges and universities during the next decade or so.
Clearly, if colleges have large numbers of staff teaching education
in B.Ed. courses, the colleges are the places to expand postgraduate
certificate work. Where does this leave the university institutes,
schools and departments of education? There must be an immediate rationalization of the work of institutes and departments
as has happened in some A.T.O.s. The separate department is
now an anachronism. A strong university staff situation will be
encouraged by the further development of schools of education
in terms of research and in terms of services to teachers (library,
resources, etc.) as at Bristol and Exeter for instance. One would
like to see 'team research' introduced, as in physical sciences, so
that university staff would work with teachers taking higher
degrees in groups. Increasingly, the School of Education will
become an administrative centre for the decentralized certificate,
B.Ed. (pre-service and in-service) degree, diploma, and postgraduate certificate, all taught and taken at the colleges of education. But of great importance will be the establishment in
every school of education of strong research and higher degree
departments.

This plan for a decade requires certain conditions to be satisfied
for its success. First, the pooling and the U.G.C. systems of
financing teacher education must be immediately reviewed.

Without necessarily interfering with the present binary system, the pooling system might continue to support the certificate work, but the schools of education, B.Ed. degree, diploma and higher degree provisions should surely be financed by earmarked grants from the D.E.S., transmitted either through the present U.G.C. or through a new Teacher Education Grants Committee. This would lead to a multiple system of financing colleges of education if the present system of control was to be retained, but it is not beyond the wit of man to devise an appropriate accounting system.

Second, the territory for schools of education (i.e. A.T.O.s) must be immediately reviewed. The country should be re-divided into regional areas each covering a similar number of schools and teachers, and arranged so that the university centre is within easy commuting distance from any of the schools. It would be most advantageous if these regional areas corresponded closely, either singly or in groups, with the territories of the new regional authorities to be set up under the reorganization of local government. As a consequence of this reorganization, some existing A.T.O.s may have to amalgamate, while others may have to divide: some universities may lose their separate A.T.O., others may gain one where they did not have one before. The object would be to provide an effective service to the schools in the area, to strengthen the possibility of a sound research centre, and to link the university with an optimum number of colleges for efficient administration bearing in mind that most colleges will grow much larger.

(b) *Short in-service courses*

The short course is one lasting from one day to two or three weeks, and can occur by release during school time, or after school, or at weekends and in vacations. Surveys show that the local authorities continue to be the chief providers of this type of course. Can they continue to organize such courses largely on their own? The D.E.S. has recently cast the A.T.O.s in the role of co-ordinators of in-service education within their areas, and this suggests an increase in the liaison and co-operation between L.E.A.s, universities and colleges. But the structural basis for this combined operation is weak. A leading difficulty is that most L.E.A.s do not appoint staff full-time to tackle in-service education on the scale required. Many authorities do not have advisors for

L

important parts of the school curriculum. There is a need too for the introduction on a wider scale of 'teacher-organizers' or 'teacher-tutors' as in Surrey or Essex for example. There is also the part to be played by the new teacher centre wardens. Unfortunately, these latter appointments are often made on a low salary scale: there is a real danger too that too much will be expected of these people, and that they will be both overworked and underpaid. New educational legislation is needed to ensure that each authority has an adequate staffing establishment for in-service education and advisory functions. Beyond this, the authorities must be required to work through co-ordinating Boards of the kind described below.

In each area, the timing/frequency and the location of short courses must be very carefully reviewed. In some localities, custom and tradition may have set a pattern that ought to be questioned. In other parts of the country, interesting arrangements have been made that should be monitored and discussed. The manner in which in-service topics are chosen must be carefully considered, not only by means of market research, but also in relation to the limitations of school timetables, to development projects and to staffing. There is the further question of the part to be played by universities and colleges: colleges of education, because of their staffing, facilities and location, will come more and more into the picture and help with short course provision and project or study-group initiatives; universities are less likely to provide short courses if they use their resources in the ways described above. It would probably be most satisfactory if the college share in this work was financed directly through fees and charges met by the organizing L.E.A.

(c) *Organization and co-ordination of in-service education*

We return to this as a key issue. Finance on the scale required may not be provided unless there is evidently a viable structure for ensuring that the money is effectively and fairly applied. Yet there remains much apathy about the solution of the problem. In the industrial field, the Training Boards were set up by special legislation to meet a felt need for in-service education, and executive education as well as tradesmen's education has been covered. The idea of a levy on the employers is not foreign to education: the training pool is subscribed in this way, and research bodies (Schools Council, N.F.E.R.) are financed by a levy on L.E.A.s plus a D.E.S. contribution, directly or indirectly. Presumably, there is scope for a modest increase in these levies, and for an increase in the D.E.S. contribution, provided the case had been made and the structure existed which could be seen to give every teacher an equal chance (apart from strategic priorities) to good in-service provision.

The suggested reorganization of local government provides an opportunity which must not be missed. National government would have to ensure that regional authorities made an equal and adequate provision for the staffing and support of short courses, linked with similar provision for local research and development. At the same time, national government would ensure (through the suggested Teacher Education Grants Committee) that the provision of courses for named qualifications was equivalent in each regional authority, perhaps by covering all the cost of tuition and secondment from the national exchequer with the university institutes/colleges recovering their running costs by charging an agreed economic fee to the exchequer. The government auditors would have to be satisfied on this point. The government might withhold this financial support in areas where the provision was not sufficiently varied or adequate.

This scheme would not work effectively without a working liaison between the regional authority and the university/college authorities. The simplest machinery would seem to be to set up statutory Boards for each regional authority area composed of say twelve members—three representing the regional authority, three representing the teachers, three representing universities/ colleges, and three representing the D.E.S. These Boards might be empowered with an executive function to ensure a balanced and adequate provision for both in-service education and research and development in the region concerned. The levy on the regional authority would be paid to the Board, and the government finance for secondment (salaries and fees) would be channelled through the Boards. It should be a statutory limitation on these Boards that they did not themselves engage in the provision of training courses or in research and development. The Board's staff would consist of executive secretary, and clerical and accounting officers. Any advisory committees set up by the Boards would consist of 'advisors' from the regional authority staff, the schools, and the universities/colleges: the Boards would have no paid advisors.

The regional Boards would cover all in-service education. Pre-service education, i.e. the certificate courses, would continue to be financed by the pool system administered by the D.E.S. The cost of administration of the schools of education, including academic salaries and grants for academic research on a scale commensurate with a university institution, would be covered by direct grants to schools of education on a three-year or five-year basis.

Conclusion

In the first part of this chapter, some cardinal principles that might be taken to form the basis of future planning were outlined. These principles were seen as guiding lines for in-service provision during the next thirty years. The changes during this period will be at least as dramatic as the changes since 1940. The ideal structure for teacher education proposed for the year 2000 embraces an old concept in new clothes—regional 'Universities of Teachers'. As members of these universities, most teachers will have taken a B.Ed. degree, and many will qualify further through diploma and higher degree courses. Research and development will be much more widespread than now, and closely linked to in-service programmes. Strong research centres with staffs of 100/200 will come to exist in each new university, and colleges of education will form the centres of such new universities, co-operating closely with schools and teachers.

This vision for the future was seen to be reached through a transition stage of ten to fifteen years. The transition stage would involve fundamental changes in the structuring and finance of in-service teacher education, Area Training Organizations would be reformed and aligned as far as possible with reorganized local authority areas. University schools of education would be rationalized, and most of the teaching decentralized to colleges of education. Regional Training Boards for In-Service Education would be set up for each region with independent constitutions: finance for in-service education would be channelled through these Boards. A Teacher Education Grants Committee would finance the university schools of education, and make grants for the running costs, secondment salaries, and research, involved in named qualification courses.

By means of this overall plan, there would emerge a new

structure for the improvement of teaching involving a partnership of teachers, authorities, universities and colleges, yet safeguarding the interests of all. It is to be hoped that the present enquiries into teacher education will recognize the urgent need for major structural changes of this kind, or some other alternative scheme, for without a radical solution the quality of teaching in British schools is likely to deteriorate: the demands of mass education in a technological society may be too great for the schools to carry.

Nine

Roland Meighan and
Peter Chambers

**The Structure of
Teacher Education**

Introduction

In view of the rigorous scrutiny to which teacher education is at
present being subjected, it is important to examine why so much
criticism exists and to ask what prospects the future holds for
its development. It is easy to find ammunition to fire at the
colleges of education and to forget the very considerable achievements made during the past decade. The rapid expansion in
numbers, the introduction of the B.Ed. degree and the shifts in
emphasis away from 'training' towards 'education' have been
carried out in a variety of ways in different colleges throughout the
country and with different degrees of success. This variety allows
for a selective, impressionistic debate and so this chapter concen-
trates on the structure of teacher education in the colleges rather
than the content of their curricula for it is believed that many of
the failures derive from the structure and that the successes have
often been in spite of it.

The implications of the structure

(a) Basic training

The present structure of teacher education can be explained by
the concepts of training on which it is based. Although the colleges
themselves may perceive their functions differently, the concept
that still predominates is that of a *basic training*. Most teachers
undergo a period of full-time training at the beginning of their
careers and any further training results from personal effort,
random local provision, experience and 'retraining' in the schools.
No further training, other than the probationary year is built into
the structure. Given that knowledge is thought to be doubling
every ten years and that the schools are in a state of flux this
would seem to be a serious weakness. It is a weakness magnified
by the increasing complexity and diversity of the teacher's role.
The concept of 'class teacher' with its notions of instruction and
passive learning has been largely superseded by 'organizer of
learning' with assumptions about active learning and varied size

teaching groups. The change has demanded new skills, different attitudes and more knowledge, yet the concept of basic training hardly takes this into account. It would probably be preferable to apply an alternative concept of *initial training* in which practitioners are expected to develop competence in a few defined skills and undertake further periods of training in order to extend these. A linked concept is that of *sandwich training*. An element of this already exists in the teaching practice periods in schools. In an initial training scheme these periods in schools might be extended so that a student could spend up to a year in school as a paid junior member of the profession with well-defined and limited responsibilities. Such a scheme deserves attention in view of the speculation about the *'retraining'* system of schools, as analysed by Perry (1969). He suggests that there are two training systems: the official college-based system and the unofficial school-based system, which functions more efficiently than the former and often produces large numbers of teachers with different approaches from those advocated by colleges. The minority of teachers who resist this latter system may well be regularly reduced in numbers by promotion to colleges, the local inspectorates and research teams. If this is the case the structure of training required needs to incorporate some way of reducing the dissonance between the two systems. An initial phase, together with further in-service periods, could do this and dispel any myths about who enjoyed the monopoly of effective teaching procedures. It would also enable teachers to keep up to date in their knowledge and skills and build these up in stages with opportunities to reflect on their theoretical bases and remain flexible in response to change based on research. A concept of *phased training* would therefore reduce the consequences of the 'retraining' system and improve the communications between colleges and schools.

(b) Concurrent training

The structure related to basic training also incorporates *concurrent training*. Although this is often used to describe the interspersing of school practice within the total college course, for the purpose of this paper it is used in the sense of holding all courses for 'personal' educational and professional education 'concurrently'. During the basic course, the academic and professional aspects develop side by side. This is justified by the belief that study in depth forms an essential part of the personal education of teachers. Yet this personal element is not required by dentists or lawyers whose depth of study is related to their professional skills. There is no reason why education should not be a similar study in depth for teachers if it were accorded more time. The further argument that secondary teachers require academic material for their specialist subjects assumes that the role of a teacher is primarily that of an instructor, yet pedagogical elements are often lacking in these courses and they rarely take into account how far the teacher's role has shifted to that of organizer, enabler or facilitator. The development of team-teaching poses further questions about the pre-eminence of personal education in the concurrent scheme.

One consequence of a structure devoted to concurrent training is the familiar division in colleges between 'academics' in main subjects and 'professionals' in education departments. It is sometimes further differentiated by similar divisions within the Education Department. Both sides are ambivalent about the demands made on college time by the periods of teaching practice that characterize the concurrent course. Wadd's analysis (1969) describes the conflicts caused by this situation and shows how the attempts to solve the problem by recruiting staff capable of contributing to both aspects at a high level is thwarted by their scarcity. A more flexible arrangement could solve this dilemma. Academic pursuits outside the study of education could be followed in the later stages of training as an option likely to appeal to secondary students. These options need not necessarily be offered in the same institution. The effects of the present situation are highlighted by the B.Ed. courses. These require a traditional academic subject as a main constituent, modelled on the 'pure' degree (Fox, 1969) whereas an 'applied' degree, e.g. as in agriculture, may well be more relevant. Most of the current proposals for teacher education (e.g. diversification into liberal arts colleges, a four-year course for a graduate profession, polyversities for professional courses, or school and teacher centre-based training) assume that concurrent training will be a fundamental element. The widespread dissatisfaction with B.Ed. courses alone suggests that some reappraisal of this rigid commitment is necessary. Experience with the single example of *consecutive* training, the postgraduate year following a three-year degree course, does not however suggest that this is an appropriate model and comparison with other professions emphasizes this. A graduate cannot be converted into doctor or lawyer through one year's professional training. In the past, he may have been able to develop competence as a subject instructor at the secondary level, but the increasing complexity of a teacher's role makes this less and less likely.

(c) *The common course*

The present structure revolves around the concept of a *common course*, the completion of which offers 'qualified teacher' status. This modern equivalent of the mediaeval '*ius ubique docendi*' allows any teacher to follow whatever professional route he chooses and become youth leader, infant teacher, secondary specialist, local organizer, head teacher or technical college lecturer providing he can get someone to employ him. There is thus the notion of embryonic omnicompetence implicit in the concept of the common course.

In practice the commitment to the common course is very much less. Many colleges are already 'multi-technics' in the sense that they put students into infant, junior and secondary groups; provide a range of main subjects and, in some circumstances, allow variations like a shortened course, or a specialism in youth leadership. Nevertheless this latter is not a requirement for obtaining a youth leader appointment and the age range grouping during training does not automatically provide entry into a similar range when teaching. The evidence rather suggests a discontinuity of professional socialization related to the staffing needs of the schools—a discontinuity fostered by the effects of 'retraining'. The serious problem is that the concept of the common course perpetuates the idea of omnicompetence and obscures the real variety of structures within the teaching profession that demand variability in training.

(d) *Role diffusion of lecturers*

The concepts of basic course, concurrent training and a common course present great difficulties for college lecturers, especially in education departments. The structure tends to make their roles diffuse to the point of contradiction (see L.M. Evans, 1970). A certificate with universal application requires a similar measure of omnicompetence in those responsible for its award. They are thus required to match up to impossible standards and may become scapegoats for structural inadequacies.

As Faragher's mock advertisement in the *Times Educational Supplement* of 10 April 1970 suggests, conflict is inherent.

WANTED: Good honours graduate with advanced diploma in education and extensive teaching experience, e.g. of the infants' school integrated day, of disadvantaged and immigrant children, of comprehensive schools with inter-disciplinary team-teaching and C.S.E. Mode 3 and of A level work.

Ability required to run unstreamed, vertically grouped classes containing honours-degree candidates, ex-sec. mod. late-developers, drop-outs from university and industry and mature students with no full-time education for 20 years. Counselling experience required since most students have either been refused registration for B.Ed. or object to taking compulsory subjects they do not intend to teach, or have pretended they wanted to teach primary children to get accepted, or simply do not want to teach.

The successful candidate will be expected to teach regularly in local schools and to read for a Higher Degree, but owing to a recent D.E.S. decision he cannot be replaced if seconded for school experience or further study. Lack of ambition is likewise an advantage since the staffing-ratio is to become less favourable; and as the annexe may soon close, and Box and Cox is discreetly buried and the intake reduced there is no chance of promotion and some chance of redundancy.

However, exciting opportunities for adventurous improvisation may arise in the next decade as more and more final solutions to the College of Education problem are formulated and surprise announcements bring conversion to interprofessional training, or liberal arts, or in-service training, or amalgamation with a polytech: or even a four-term year to meet the unforeseen shortage of secondary teachers resulting from

r.s.l.a. and late-leaving in comprehensive schools,
together with compulsory training for graduates
and a lack of male applicants to colleges of
education.

To avoid criticism of the resultant situation, it is
expected that the successful candidate will accept
a five-year tenure and thereafter revert to school-
teaching or retreat to a university education
department.

A phased system might well reduce this role conflict since each
phase could specify and limit its objectives and staff would be
appointed accordingly. A lecturer servicing the initial phase
would not necessarily contribute to the third or fourth phase
(e.g. a Head Teachers' Training Course) unless he had some
expertise in this field to offer.

(e) *Selection of students*

The recent history of teacher shortage allied to the present
structure has presented problems of the age of entry. Although
most students are eighteen years of age, it is frequently suggested
that this is too young. The situation is further complicated by
the very proper concern for a high level of entry qualifications.
At present, approximately one-third of entrants have two 'A
levels', a further third one 'A level' and the remainder five 'O
levels' or the equivalent. This concern for high standards is
a necessary prerequisite of a structure that dispatches qualified
teachers to the schools at the age of twenty-one. The alarm
about teacher education losing its proportion of the highly
qualified with the expansion of higher education extrapolated
into 1981 (see A.T.C.D.E., 1970) is indicative of how critical this
is. It would be less important in a phased system. The initial stage
could serve as a *selection device* and qualifications for entry at
each stage would legitimately vary. The entry of mature students
would also benefit from this more flexible system. At present
these entrants may either go to a special day college or join the
school leavers in the other colleges to take the three-year course.
Even when reductions in the length of the course are made they
create both personal and administrative difficulties. A phased
system could cater for their varieties of experience and allow

variable entry according to previous experience and qualifications
by permitting candidates to miss intermediate phases or parts of
phases. It would also reduce the dependence of the profession on
external selectors. A recent study by Isaac (1970) has demonstrated
the weakness of this system by showing how misleading G.C.E.
results can be. The high failure rate in B.Ed. qualifying examinations by candidates who had previously been rejected by universities when compared with others of higher aspiration levels
indicates the greater validity of allocation by internal selectors.
Thus many of the expressed difficulties of entrance and selection
can be explained in structural terms.

(f) *Wastage*

Nowhere can this be more clearly illustrated than by reference to
wastage. Quite apart from the difficulties of getting men candidates
willing to undertake attending vocational commitment at the age
of seventeen, the subsequent wastage is one of the most striking
features of the profession. There are three main types: wastage
during the course of training; wastage on course completion; and
wastage after a short teaching career.

The wastage during training is perhaps the least serious.
Estimates of 10 per cent over three years have been made. It
would appear reasonable that since the bulk of this occurs in the
first year it can be accepted as a selection element within the
course of training.

However, in 1968, 18½ per cent of the students who qualified as
teachers did not take up teaching appointments. Eight and a half
per cent, mainly women, did not enter any employment at all,
but the remaining 10 per cent took up pensionable posts other
than in schools. Some further light is thrown on these figures by
a study of teachers in training by Smithers and Carlisle (1970).
Just over half of their sample of students in the final year of
training indicated an ideal preference for something other than
teaching. It may be assumed that some of these took appropriate
action and make up most of the wastage that takes place immediately after qualifying.

The wastage of serving teachers is also notable. In 1966, 22,000
women joined the teaching force but 20,000 left. This net gain of
2,000 is a peak figure as the previous years all showed smaller
gains. The wastage is higher for men and women below thirty

years of age. Thus after three years of training, a sizeable minority pursue a teaching career of even shorter duration. The Plowden Report was content that this high rate of turnover meant a constant flow of fresh ideas into schools and could be tolerated in the hope of later returns to teaching. Such a light dismissal of the problem can only be deplored.

Again, the current structure and concepts of training appear to be influential. A phased system of training with a shorter initial period could make a considerable impact. Wastage would still occur, but in relation to shorter, differential periods of training. More flexible recruitment at each phase would regularize the return of teachers and although there can be no hard evidence that this would improve teacher supply it would hardly make it worse! Certainly there would be a saving in economic terms.

(g) *Research and development*

Structural changes could improve the opportunities for *research* and *innovation*. At present this is undertaken by a number of agencies. The major source of educational research would appear to be the University Schools of Education, the Schools Council, the N.F.E.R. and the Nuffield Foundation. The colleges' contribution may well be frequent and widespread but it is mainly through individual lecturers working for further degrees or personal satisfaction, and small-scale exercises by students, especially for B.Ed. It is however little reported and rarely collated. This is surely a reflection of the need to develop so much knowledge and so many skills in students in the very short time available. Yet, if the colleges are to be vanguards of the best practices in teaching and innovators in educational practice through rigorous and intensive research, then opportunities for developing this sector of their activities need to be created. Unless there is a greatly reduced staff/student ratio, structural changes which define the tutor's function more clearly and allow easier exchange between schools and colleges present the most favourable way of permitting this commitment to innovation. In particular, research could be a prominent feature of the later phases of training. The choice of staff for these phases would be influenced by their experience in educational research and the selection of students be governed by their research orientations. Allied to their experience in schools, their period as research students would present a notable spearhead for research in education that would be essentially practical and also enrich the teaching in both colleges and schools.

(h) *Students in residence*

Finally, although the question of *residential training* need not be a structural problem, the tradition is so deeply rooted as to appear related.

The Robbins Committee reported that in 1962, 70 per cent of all college of education students were in residence. By 1967–8, this proportion had fallen to 44 per cent with a further 31 per cent in lodgings. In this way, the traditions of closely-knit residential communities have been drastically and suddenly changed. The increase in size has been a contributory factor. Whereas in 1958–9, only three colleges had more than 500 students, in 1969–70 there were just over 100 such colleges and eighteen with more than 1,000 students. The notion of living in a community has been greatly weakened by these two changes which have occurred in response to the need to increase the supply of teachers as rapidly and cheaply as possible. Whether the expansion realized these hopes is open to question. As Price (1969) shows, the cost effectiveness argument is suspect since the differences in overall costs of colleges of 200 students and those of 1,000 are hardly significant compared with the variability in costs of colleges of similar size. Evidence from industrial sociology (see R. Cooper, 1965) suggests that large organizations have disadvantages. They have, for example, administrative problems created by inefficient communication and they produce personal problems for their members by weakening their sense of identity. In colleges, this is borne out by Shipman's study (1969), in which he suggests that the single central focus of studies, the training of teachers, becomes less apparent with increases in size. Since this unifying focus is also weakened by the concurrent elements of the academic and professional parts of a long basic course, it is clear that structural changes are imperative. Whereas the teaching function of the informal organization of the small residential college did much to provide a unifying core to a diverse series of courses, the informal organization of a large college, dedicated to the diversification of activities, is hardly likely to do the same. It is argued therefor that the commitment to residence and community is no longer so relevant and that phased training with its increasing professional contacts can provide the coherence and unity that is being lost.

(i) *Summary*

This account of the concepts and traditions of teacher education has attempted to demonstrate that the present structure does not cater for the changes that have taken place in the teacher's role. The increasing demand for teachers to possess highly sophisticated and diverse skills necessitates structural changes in teacher education. A structure that would offer initial training and phased in-service training as part of the career pattern of all teachers would seem more appropriate than one based on the concepts of basic training, with short spells of practice teaching in a concurrent, common course, which leads to a universal 'licence to teach'. Such a change in structure would help to delineate and clarify the objectives of the different phases of training and thus reduce role conflict among the teacher educators. It is further estimated that such a system would reduce wastage in the profession, allow for a more flexible system of entry into it and improve mobility and communication between its various parts. It would also present a scheme more suited to the even more explosive changes that are likely to take place in the future. The cumulative effects of earlier change in relation to the structure of the teaching profession and to the patterns of higher education mean that the training of student teachers must include still more preparation for change. It will therefore be necessary to indicate some of these likely changes before describing the precise form that the structure of teacher education should take.

Preparation for change and the changing situation

Perhaps the most important areas of education in which change is likely to have the most telling effect on the structure of teacher education are those of the teacher's role and the organization of schools; the provision of in-service training; the changing methods of teaching in higher education; the relationships of schools and colleges; and the relationships between teachers and taught. All of these are likely to stretch the resources of the present structure, but equally are also capable of facilitating the provision of alternative structures that can meet the needs and responsibilities of teacher education in a highly dynamic age.

The structure of the teaching profession

The first area concerns the nature of the teacher's task. The concept of the common course and the existing Burnham salary scales obscure the real complexity of the *Teaching Profession*. Within the Education Service it is possible to find individuals who with no further training after their initial course are employed as youth leaders, head teachers, college lecturers, local inspectors, housemasters or remedial teachers. 'Sitting with Nellie', once so scornfully dismissed as a method of training, is still a major form for those teachers who are going to do something more than conventional teaching. Yet, as Eric Hoyle (1969, p. 61) points out, these are the majority and the holders of graded posts and above outnumber assistant teachers. Further, the complexity of the assistant teacher's role means a whole range of additional skills can be added to those he is expected to perform on completion of his basic training. These role sectors will include elements related to classroom teaching, administration, remedial teaching, guidance and diagnosis, training and social welfare. It can be reasonably expected that the career structure of the profession will oblige young teachers to develop some of these sectors, but the skills required cannot be obtained satisfactorily from the present sources: common, basic course, experience, or pot-luck in in-service training. There is therefore a case for removing the elements of chance and building such training courses into the structure of professional education. Later phases designed to develop such special courses and which offered a related qualification, e.g. a B.Ed. in educational administration, could meet this need. With these sorts of skills and qualifications in mind the structure could also provide initiating roles for professional educators. The lack of these in the teaching profession contrasts markedly with other professions (e.g. house man in medicine, articled clerk in the law) and may represent one element in the comparatively low status afforded to it. If teachers were to play a part in organizing initiating roles for young teachers it would increase the amount of self-determination given to the profession. The present system of a probationary year is a poor substitute, for as Cornwell has indicated it has a variety of forms and little structure. Indeed one of the major sources of professional help is the fellow probationer (*T.E.S.*, 15 November 1963).

The changing roles of teachers

The inadequacy of the present structure is most clearly revealed by an analysis of the ways in which *a teacher's role* is changing. B. Bernstein (1967) summarizes this succinctly. He suggests that an increasingly 'open society' with an expanding technology and a rapid increase in total knowledge, requires a different type of school where the teachers, rather than being 'instructors', are enablers, facilitators, problem posers, catalysts or *organizers of learning*. Thus, in addition to the increasing complexity of the role sectors, there is a change in the central role focus, which reduces the contribution of imitation in professional socialization. The instructional models that students and young teachers remember from their own schooldays are no longer so relevant and the changes also affect the help and guidance experienced teachers can give. The introduction of team-teaching and the widespread acceptance of progressive education based on the various forms of discovery learning (in spite of the cries of woe from the contributors to the Black Papers) are symptomatic of these changes in role. By and large, the colleges are fully aware of these changes but the pressures of the common course and the short time available for training preclude adequate investigation of such innovations in school let alone the appropriate training approaches to help students prepare for them. The trends towards 'open schools' and child-centred education have reduced the role distance between teachers and taught and this, too, has led to further role changes. The skills that allow acceptable instrumental leadership in classrooms committed to children participating in decision-making in the best democratic traditions are markedly different from those required by even the most benevolent of authoritarian instructors. Yet it is difficult for these issues to be reflected in the curricula of the colleges of education. It is hardly their fault. Given concurrent academic and professional training only a limited amount of time can be given to the study of education. Academic B.Ed. courses limit the opportunity still further. If, instead of a B.Ed. with half the qualification in geography or English, it was possible to study educational technology or the teaching of reading, in depth and detail, then there would be real provision of groups of teachers able to direct and facilitate the changes in role that the 'new' teaching situations require. Such B.Ed. courses would be a legitimate element in the phased structure that has been proposed.

M

The changing schools

Many of these 'new' ideas are, however, not new at all, but the difference between pioneering and establishing practices, and between ideas based first on a 'hunch' and then, later, on more scientific grounds is crucial. Innovation is one thing: diffusion another. It is this widespread *diffusion* of different methods of organization and curriculum development that is essentially novel, particularly in the light of the massive publicity that comes from education being news not only to increasingly well-informed parents, but also to the mass media and the politicians.

Thus, in recent years, teachers have had to adapt to comprehensive schools, to large schools, to mixed schools, to open-plan schools, to family grouping, to programmed learning, to new methods of teaching reading, to new maths, to Nuffield Science, to middle schools, to curriculum packs, to related studies, to team-teaching and to educational technology. This list may seem formidable, but it is not even complete.

The response to these innovations in schools has been an enormous increase in the objectives set by the colleges of education and their curricula have reflected these increases. In a ferment of activity, the colleges have developed curriculum courses, reorganized their professional groupings, introduced integrative courses and scrutinized their existing schemes. But, even with the best will in the world, the process has been one of accretion, rather than selection. A structure which reiterates the notion of a common course and concurrent training stymies radical innovation by limiting the time to do it. The parable of new wine and old bottles is surely apposite!

One radical approach that has favour is that of diversifying colleges by making them liberal arts colleges or parts of polytechnics. This is seductive, as it would appear to offer the opportunity to increase the range of courses selectively and allow students to concentrate their studies in the context of broad-based institutions. It is however also likely to reduce the teacher education element in training at a time when the changing nature of schools demands an increase! On the other hand, a phased system would allow training to cater for those innovations and prepare the student teacher for them as his competence and experience developed. It would mean that there was a constant influx of students into the colleges at various phases in their careers who were fresh from the schools and also able to reflect on existing practices and the consequences of innovatory theory. This would develop institutional interaction of a kind that would minimize the divisions within the profession and create the opportunities for an 'Education Profession' of the kind valued by Hoyle (*op. cit.*, pp. 67–70).

In-service training and teachers' centres

Another change that has important implications for the structure of teacher education has been the growth of *teachers' centres*. In the last eight years there has been a remarkable expansion from a situation in which there were but two or three in large boroughs to the present provision in which almost all Local Education Authorities have a centre. Their functions are various but they still retain the impetus given to them for *Research and Curriculum Development* (1967). They provide in-service training, short courses, teaching aids services, workshops and other meetings for teachers. All of this is commendable and it has contributed to innovation in schools, but the staff tend to be isolated and their development schemes contribute little to initial training, except when the college campus also houses the centre. Experience of combined college teachers' centre establishments indicates that not only is their work a legitimate area for the colleges of education to develop but the combination is of mutual benefit to initial training and to the diffusion of curriculum development schemes. The colleges can provide the facilities for curriculum development and in-service training and the necessary professional contacts for the centre tutors. Where colleges are badly placed geographically, there could be an appropriate staff relationship with the nearest college and the criteria for staff appointments could follow very similar lines. This would allow easy exchange and mutual support. The *in-service training element* is of particular interest since many colleges have been reducing their range of one-year supplementary courses without replacing them with the short courses popularized by the teachers' centres. Some colleges do, of course, have such schemes but when these are in competition with those provided by the teachers' centre, they represent a potential waste of resources and an area of inter-professional conflict that may mar the relationships between colleges and schools. The phased structure would allow for considerable rationalization of in-service training and its attendant curriculum development projects. By basing these services on the colleges and linking their staff, the quality of initial training is likely to rise. If the colleges' activities are to be diversified, the extension of their areas of competence along these lines is more likely to benefit the schools than any proposal to diversify their activities to form liberal arts colleges, or multivarsities.

Changing methods in higher education

Whereas the previous changes are seen as making structural change necessary, there are changes taking place that are more important because they will facilitate changes in the structure of teacher education. Among these are innovations in further and higher education. These include *modular systems* of organization and evaluation, *educational technology, programmed learning*, and *computerization.*

The most prominent example of how these changes are being utilized is in the *Open University*, which may be the prototype of a major part of the higher education of the future. Here the course will consist of a series of learning experiences, including a correspondence phase, a radio phase, a television phase, short residential courses, and part-time attendance at a study centre. A given course may include all or some of these phases in varying proportions and sequences. Many elements will be common to a variety of courses. This system would appear to have the advantages of relative flexibility, economy and efficiency in respect of time, money resources and manpower. Included are the other elements listed above. It offers a model for the structuring of teaching and education and may indeed provide one major source for elements in the different phases of training, e.g. the academic content for a secondary teacher, the educational |psychology for a remedial advisor, or the refresher material for a married woman wishing to return to teaching.

Educational technology implies a systematic use of teaching aids and the rigorous programming of learning to produce efficient and effective education. The recognition of the interrelated parts of learning theory, the applications of flow systems and critical path analysis and the development of integrated systems of objectives, instruction and evaluation will be a prerequisite of a new structure with concepts of initial training and consequent in-service phases. As analysed by B. Hopson (1966) the application of educational technology to teacher education will produce the flexible system of training appropriate to the multi-faceted nature of the teacher's role. Perhaps the most useful innovation for the structure envisaged is, however, the *module system*. It implies that any total course includes many self-contained sub-courses, which can be self-sufficient in terms of specific objectives and modes of evaluation. The completion of a modular course thus involves the satisfactory completion of a specified number of sub-courses, or modules. The sequence of courses can be predetermined and alternatives can be made available. Opportunities for exchange between institutions can be offered and the phasing of the course can become very flexible indeed. Experience of such schemes in the U.S.A. has shown the value of the modular 'transcript' and the phased system would lend itself to this approach. Each student would have a 'transcript' and amass the appropriate modules for completion of his initial course. To this could be added modules describing a prescribed period of paid practical teaching and the relevant in-service training modules for the particular career structure the student wished to follow. The system of credits used by the Open University is similar in intent and could be incorporated into the structure.

The linking of *computers* into this system with central information and item data banks is a likely further development. Not only would this facilitate the administration of qualifications and courses and their evaluation, it would also allow any person at any stage in his life or education to obtain information about the options open to him, both locally and nationally. From this, he could have this information programmed to individual specifications for study facilities and curricular content. Far from being the inhibiting 'Big Brother', this could increase individual choice in education to a far greater extent than is at present possible.

The flexibility of such system and the ease with which it could make *adaptation* or retraining its goals would ensure that the structural changes proposed would be relevant for the 1980s and 1990s. It would not require much ingenuity for the programme to compensate for the cultural and integrative benefits that were provided by the basic course in the small residential colleges between 1930 and 1950.

Relationships with the schools and the involvement of teachers in training

Whatever structure emerges in teacher education, it will have to provide for much greater *involvement by teachers in the training*. It is the least a profession can demand and as the numbers of teachers required has grown and the sizes of classes declined, the number of school practice places, especially in the large conurbations, has reached saturation point. There can be few teachers who have not had the experience of having a student in his or her class. This involvement by teachers in teaching practice and in the probationary year has led to considerable criticism about the links between schools and colleges. It has culminated in the pressure for the professional aspects of teacher training to be the responsibility of teachers in schools. The criticisms about the lack of research and in-service training already discussed are not however the main charges. The main allegation is that the colleges are inefficient in producing adequately qualified teachers. This is probably the least justifiable charge as within the weaknesses of the present structure the colleges emerge with more credit than discredit. Certainly, the most frequently praised sector of the education system is the primary section, almost entirely staffed and developed by the products of the colleges; whereas the areas that are allegedly most worthy of criticism are those of secondary and higher education, which recruit the bulk of their staff elsewhere and train them on the site themselves. The involvement of schools in teaching practice has often been marked in the past by some degree of suspicion, but the present record is one of close co-operation and shared responsibility. As this co-operation has increased *the interdependence of school and college* has become more manifest. It is, however, the evidence of the probationary year, the schools' major involvement in training, that challenges most strongly the call to let professional training pass entirely into the hands of the schools. With honourable exceptions the schools appear to have abdicated a large share of their responsibilities by careless allocation of classes, inadequate or inconsistent support and exaggerated expectations. Indeed, is has been known for a probationer, with a difficult class, to act as host for a student on teaching practice. As Cornwell (*op. cit.*, 1963) suggests it is often the good sense of probationers and the wisdom of individual heads and authorities that represent the saving graces of the present probationary system. As it is, the general impression is one of retraining new entrants into passive conformity, especially at the secondary level.

Indicative of the poor communication between schools and colleges is the second part of the case that college lecturers are no longer able to contribute to professional training because they no longer teach children. Yet most members of college staffs are appointed because they have rich experience in schools. It is a symptom of the degree of commitment to this ideal that the colleges' professional journal, *Education for Teaching*, has featured an article on how recent changes have made this ideal difficult to attain (S. J. Eggleston, 1966). The present criticisms would appear to demand that tutors demonstrate constantly their ability with children although the specific objectives of this expertise are rarely stated. A more sensible demand would be that lecturers should be involved in development and research in schools with teachers rather than be seeking constant re-experience for its own sake.

The assumption underlying the demand for more school control is that the present practice in school is sound and worthy of emulation and that it offers an appropriate testing ground. In view of the state of flux of the school curriculum this poses several questions, not least being the traditional autonomy of the individual school. One feature that the colleges can offer is a consistent reference against which various school experiences can be evaluated. This is brought home convincingly by an examination of the effects of the present variety of school experiences on students' performances (K. G. Collier, 1959). A 'poor' school produced a poor mark; a 'good' school a better one. Major modifications are necessary to offset differential effect but these would reach enormous proportions if the schools were to have sole responsibility for training. Worse, the relevance of college theoretical courses may become extremely tenuous. It is therefore argued that both parties must be fully involved in training and that the relationships between schools and colleges should be co-operative, sympathetic, flexible and mutually critical. That the recent emphasis has been on criticism rather than sympathy is a reflection of how inadequate a short, basic, common course is as a preparation for a lifelong career in teaching. The interspersing of theoretical work and practical teaching in a phased 'sandwich' structure would not only reduce this inadequacy but it would also clarify what was expected from the two partners and the student at a given phase of training. It would help to reduce the status differential by accepting the separate but interdependent aspects of theory and practice, deny the divisive elements of 'retraining' and improve the communication between schools and colleges. In short, it could only improve the relationships within the education profession.

Interpersonal relationships

Finally, the *democratization* of schools and colleges is another striking feature of change in education. The reduction of role distance, as has already been suggested, puts greater emphasis on instrumental authority in teachers and tutors and less on authoritarian role playing (Chambers, 1970). It has meant that all teachers have had to develop new *interpersonal skills* drawing from their own personal resources as opposed to the institutions in which they teach. They have needed to develop greater sensitivity to people's needs, to feedback from learning and to contextual influences on each individual. Such changes have brought stress and anxiety to the teacher's and the tutor's role. It is revealed in the increasing amount of participation by students in college government and pupils in school curriculum decisions and perhaps even more importantly in the reactions: the strength of feeling about professional standards revealed in the important super-ficialities of dress, hair cuts and punctuality. The confused situations which have produced the Radical Students' Alliance and Pupils' Councils, progressive participation and reactionary movements have far-reaching consequences for teacher training. Among the results of increased student participation in college government has been a clamour for more practical, professional training. The voice has not always been consistent, which reflects the 'anomie' described above, but it has become louder. The tutor's role diffusion exaggerated by the existing concurrent structure makes consistent answer difficult. The result is to produce further confusion, creating conflict for students as well as lecturers. The clarification that would result from structural changes as outlined would reduce many of the inconsistencies. This should help students find the instrumental authority they need to adapt to teaching in a democratic school. Stress and anxiety create their own authoritarianism. By reducing the demands of omnicompetence and tailoring the phases of training to the required levels of competence; by giving acceptable professional tasks and the necessary support to each teacher according to his phase of training, the structure would allow students and teachers to develop the self-knowledge and self-confidence to act as effective leaders in the flexible, essentially democratic learning situations that are now integral to the education scene.

Summary

In order to give adequate preparation for change, the structure of teacher education will have to be flexible, variable and differential. It will have to cater for the various sectors of the teacher's role at different stages in his career. It will have to build in ways of ensuring full and rigorous techniques of educational innovation, research and development. It will gain enormously by assuming that in-service training and curriculum development is an essential part of its task. It will have to ensure that it does not threaten the unity of the profession and it must offer a model that is appropriate for a democratic schools' system in a democratic society. By drawing on the development of educational technology and modular organization of courses, it can meet these needs as long as the structure recognizes that training is a continuous process involving initial courses and carefully related, consequent in-service provision with appropriate experiences in school for student teachers as paid practitioners to back it up.

A proposed structure for teacher education

If the changes that have taken place in schools and higher educa-tion operate in this way against a structure based on a three-year common course of basic training in monotechnic teacher colleges committed to concurrent training, an alternative structure must be found. In view of the skill and expertise already developed by the existing teacher educators, even within the inadequacies of the structure, a new structure should be able to capitalize on this foundation. These pages do not after all describe a story of failure but an account of real success in the face of very great odds. For this reason alone, structures that do not retain the central focus, i.e. preparation for teaching, are considered wasteful and inade-quate. The new structure should be concerned with the professional education of teachers to the exclusion of peripheral activities that would obscure its unity of purpose. The concept that should shape the structure should be that of *phased* professional training based on a short initial period with *sandwich* elements of teaching experience and in-service courses as an integral part of the career patterns of teachers. The phasing of the training would be related to the aspirations of the would-be teachers, the various professional commitments they intended to undertake, the different professional roles available and their qualifications and experience on entry. Such a system would incorporate selection procedures, avenues for mobility and promotion, and ways of introducing, disseminating and evaluating innovation and research. It would offer a solution to the problems caused by the present pattern of wastage and facilitate re-entry into the profession. In-service training would be directly related to initial training and the introduction of a modular system would permit training courses to initiate change as well as help adjustment to it. It would also allow training to take place in a variety of institutions and make optimum use of existing plant and resources. It would thus guarantee the maximum amount of institutional and professional flexibility.

A college system of a restructured nature would readily adjust to any of these changes, whereas the present system would not. Thus the restructuring of the colleges could be seen as an intermediate stage in an overall change of the system if and when it occurred. It would have the advantages of a logical matching of training to job specification; it would allow complete professional autonomy; and make use of the existing funds of knowledge and experience that have so long been dedicated to the training and professional advancement of teachers. Above all by opening the doors to graduate status for all teachers without granting it automatically it would ensure that degrees in education would be essentially 'applied' and 'professional' in nature, without losing parity of esteem with other degree courses. Then would the profession of education have come of age!

A possible scheme might follow these lines:

Table 11 *A proposed structure for teacher education*

SCHOOL LEAVERS   MATURE STUDENTS/
POSTGRADUATES

Year   *Typical Age*

1   ⌐————INITIAL COURSE————⌐   18

2   *Phase in schools* as School Assistants   19
                            (minimum 1 year)

3   STAGE II COURSE (exempted under   20
                              certain conditions)

4   *Phase in schools* as School Assistants Grade 2   21
                            (minimum 1 year)

5   ⌐————B.Ed. Phase————⌐   22

       PRESENT CERTIFICATED TEACHERS ENTRY

Degrees in *Classroom Practice*—(Teaching Techniques or subjects) or in *Educational Administration* or in *College Practice*

6   *Phase in schools* or *administration* or *colleges* as   23
appropriate (minimum 1 year)

7   ⌐————M.Ed. Phase————⌐   24

On similar basis to B.Ed. degree courses

8   *Phase in schools* or *Administration* or *Colleges*   25
                            (minimum 1 year)

9   ⌐————Ph.D. Phase————⌐   26

In addition refresher courses, conversion courses, additional diploma courses could be provided within this structure.

The system would be based on modules and make maximum use of educational technology as in the Open University system.

References

A.T.D.C.E. (1970), *Higher Education and Preparation for Teaching*.

Bernstein, B. (1967), 'Open schools, open society', in *New Society*, 14 September.

Chambers, R. (1970), 'Leadership and social skills in personal relationships', in *Centre 2*, Walsall, March.

Collier, K. G. (1959),'The criteria of assessment', in *Education for Teaching*, February.

Committee on Higher Education (1962), *Higher Education* (Robbins Report), H.M.S.O.

Cooper, R. (1965), 'The psychology of organizations', in *New Society*, 22 April.

Cornwell, J., *et al.*, (1963), University of Birmingham Colleges of Education Research Group, 'Teachers in their first year', in *Times Educational Supplement*, 15 November.

D.E.S. (1968-9), *Statistics in Education*.

Eggleston, S. J. (1966), 'The staffing of the Education Department', in *Education for Teaching*.

Evans, L. M. (1970), 'The master of method', in *Froebel Journal*, No. 16, March.

Faragher, M. (1970), 'Wanted', in *Times Educational Supplement*, 10 April.

Fox, D. (1969), 'What kind of degree is the B.Ed.?', in *Education for Teaching*, Summer.

Hopson, B. (1966), 'Modernizing university teaching', in *New Society*, 1 December.

Hoyle, E. (1969), 'Professional stratification and anomie in the teaching profession', in *Paedagogica Europaea*, Vol. V, Chambers.

Isaac, J. (1970), 'Social origins of trainee teachers', in *Higher Education Journal*, Vol. 17, No. 3, 1970.

Perry, L. R. (1969), 'Training', in *Education for Teaching*, Summer, No. 79.

Price, G. (1969), 'Economics and the size of colleges', in *Education for Teaching*, Summer.

Schools Council (1967), *Curriculum Development, Teachers' Groups and Centres*, Working Paper No. 10, H.M.S.O.

Shipman, M. D. (1969), 'Participation and staff relations', in *Higher Education Society Monograph*.

Smithers, A., and Carlisle, S. (1970), 'Reluctant Teachers', in *New Society*, 5 March.

Wadd, K. (1969), 'A source of conflict in colleges of education', in *Education for Teaching*, Spring.